CREATIVE BIBLE LESSONS IN JOB

A FRESH LOOK AT FOLLOWING JESUS

DOUG RANCK

CREATIVE BIBLE LESSONS
IN JOB

A FRESH LOOK AT FOLLOWING JESUS
PERFECT FOR SUNDAY SCHOOL, YOUTH MEETINGS, SMALL GROUPS, AND MORE!

DOUG RANCK

 ZONDERVAN®

 ZONDERVAN.com/
AUTHORTRACKER
follow your favorite authors

 youth
specialties

Creative Bible Lessons in Job: A Fresh Look at Following Jesus
Copyright 2008 by Youth Specialties

Youth Specialties resources, 300 S. Pierce St., El Cajon, CA 92020, are published by Zondervan, 5300 Patterson S.E., Grand Rapids, MI 49530.

Library of Congress Cataloging-in-Publication Data

Ranck, Doug.
  Creative Bible lessons in Job : a fresh look at following Jesus / Doug Ranck.
    p. cm.
  ISBN-10: 0-310-27219-X (pbk.)
  ISBN-13: 978-0-310-27219-9 (pbk.)
  1. Bible. O.T. Job—Study and teaching. I. Title.
  BS1430.55.R36 2008
  223'.100712—dc22

2007039359

Cover design by SharpSeven Design
Interior design by Mark Novelli - IMAGO MEDIA, David Conn

Printed in the United States of America

07 08 09 10 11 12 13 14 15 • 16 15 14 13 12 11 10 9 8 7 6 5 4 3 2 1

DEDICATION

To Nancy, Kelly, Landon, and Elise, who bring great joy and strength to my life.

To Alyssa, a bright, loving 15-year-old who lived life to its fullest and left too early.

TABLE OF CONTENTS

INTRODUCTION
THE POINT AND PURPOSE OF THIS BOOK

The book of Job is found among the *wisdom books* in the Bible (along with Psalms, Proverbs, Ecclesiastes, and Song of Songs), and it reminds us that living a right life is rooted in the wisdom of God, while living wrongly is rooted in disobedience and foolishness. Although the book begins and ends with a narrative, the primary literary structure of Job is poetry. It's been acknowledged by many scholars as one of the finest literary works of all time.

There are two dates associated with the book of Job. One relates to the man named Job and his historical setting, which most believe occurred during the time of the patriarchs (2000–1800 BC), and well before the time of the kings (1050–586 BC). The second date relates to the writing of the book, which many believe is anywhere from the time of Solomon's reign to the time of Nebuchadnezzar's conquest of Judah and the subsequent exile of a large number of its people to Babylon (970–605 BC). The book's author is unknown, but we can guess it was an Israelite, since the covenant name for God—*Yahweh*—is used frequently.

When you hear the name *Job,* what's the first word that comes to mind? If you answer *suffering*, you join a large cast of people who'd answer the same way. Suffering is a prevalent theme within the book, so we're quick to refer to Job or study this book of the Bible whenever suffering is the focus. However, in addition to the story of Job, his family, his interactions with his friends, and his response to God, we find truths and wisdom beyond this one theme.

The sessions in this book, although not exhaustive, will move you beyond the basic questions of *Why does God allow suffering?* and *How do I get through a time of suffering?* to the overall idea that loving and being loved unconditionally by a just, compassionate, sovereign, and merciful God provides us with hope and direction in a world that doesn't always deliver justice or happiness.

Our world is full of uncertainty and inevitable pain—for some people more than others—and the challenges we face in this life offer far more questions than answers. In a caring youth ministry, students will feel comfortable asking the hard questions. The story of Job reminds us of our limitations in the presence of an almighty God. It also assures us that it's okay to be sad, upset, and even angry about the events we experience, and it presents a God whose greatness transcends all that the world throws our way—a God who opens his arms wide to love his children.

Before you begin leading this study, be sure to strap on your seatbelt and prepare to receive teenagers' difficult yet insightful questions. Be ready to keep your students focused on the *power of God*, instead of on the people or experiences that seem more powerful when we're in the midst of a crisis. Pray for the wisdom to answer and respond to your students as God leads. Learn from Job's friends: You don't have to have all the answers, and you should listen more and speak less.

Another way to prepare is by spending some extra time in God's presence and letting him encourage and lead you. The enemy wants you to feel discouraged, but God desires to bless you and give you joy. Throughout this series may your *life verse* resonate with Job as he said, "I know that my Redeemer lives, and that in the end he will stand upon the earth" (Job 19:25).

To aid you in the teaching process, each of the 12 sessions is divided into sections that will help you move your students through a sequence of engagement, reflection, learning, and application. These sections are described below.

Leader Prep is designed to inspire you to do a little background research and plan more fully. A few basic facts or ideas for further study are offered to provide you with a larger context. I realize that many youth leaders don't have the luxury of extra time to devote to exhaustive preparation. Many are volunteers who work full time and willingly give up their free time to train and love students. Even fulltime youth leaders are stretched in many different areas. So this portion gives the leader a head start.

The Main Idea describes the purpose of the session. You'll find this to be the most useful section. Keep it in mind while you're teaching and it'll keep the group focused, while still allowing some flexibility. Translation: If you don't like some of the ideas, feel free to try your own; but at least cover the main point!

Materials You'll Need lists the items used during the session. Having your supplies ready ahead of time is always a good idea. (So you won't have to excuse yourself as you run out the door to find supplies!)

For Starters gets students interested in the topic and also gets them thinking about **The Main Idea**. In this section you're *selling* them on why they should be interested in hearing more. You'll have two options to choose from in each session. **Option 1** will require a bit more preparation and materials. It may also require a little more time. If you have an active group, this may be the choice for you. **Option 2** is geared more toward a discussion format, perfect for a group that likes to start off more slowly or for a smaller group.

Reflection will help students not only do the activities, but also think about the significance and implications of the issues they've just uncovered. In our busy culture, reflection has become a lost art. Earpieces are in, cell phones are turned on, and teenagers easily move on without pause. So this section helps students assimilate the facts as they're learning them.

Transition Statements aren't meant to imply you don't know what to say to your students! On the contrary, we know you're fully capable of letting God speak through you. These statements merely offer an idea of what you might say to lead students from one part of the session to another, just to keep things flowing. Again, if it doesn't fit your style, then go with the main point and be your own writer. You can do it!

Discover is the section where students will open their Bibles and encounter the truths God has for them in any given passage. Our intention is to let the Scripture speak into students' lives, rather than trying to prove or disprove some preconceived notions about a particular passage. This curriculum offers a guide for helping students make their own discoveries. It's recommended that you actually have students open their Bibles. The Creative Bible Lessons series offers you the opportunity to teach the Word of God and help students become comfortable and familiar with it. While media or Scripture handouts may seem more convenient, using the actual Book will be more beneficial in teenagers' long-term Christian growth.

Translation, Please! How often have we been exposed to a biblical passage without fully uncovering its meaning? Another word we might use in place of *translation* is *interpretation*. In this section students will have the opportunity to look at the facts and more fully understand the meaning for their lives today. Don't let students get away with their typical "Sunday school" answers ("Jesus," "God," "the Bible," "pray," "love my Mom and Dad," and so on). This section is designed to help students go beyond the simplistic answers we're all tempted to offer to hurting people. It's also intended to challenge your group beyond the church vocabulary they might comprehend at the exclusion of their unchurched friends. Seize the opportunity to stretch their thinking and put the truth into understandable concepts.

Making It Work is a section that could also be called *Lab*. What better time to practice a new or reaffirmed truth than with our peers? This portion gives students the opportunity—through case studies and other activities—to rehearse the application of a real-life principle. While there's no illusion of real life in these activities, the focus will at least encourage students to *imagine* putting the truth into practice.

So What? Every student should be able to answer the question, "So what?" at the end of your teaching time. If they can't, then your session was too abstract or the truth wasn't worthy of application. By answering this question for your students, they'll understand there's much to be gained from living out these biblical truths.

A FINAL WORD

The biggest theme in Job is how to deal with hard times and tragedy, so a good portion of this curriculum deals with those subjects as well. If some of your students are going through difficult times or have recently suffered great losses, it's a good idea to take their feelings and emotions into consideration as you set the tone of your meetings.

GOD, SATAN, AND US

SESSION 1: JOB 1:1-12; 2:1-6

LEADER PREP

From Genesis to Revelation, we learn about God through his words, his actions, and his interaction with the people he created. On the surface it would seem that all we need to know about God is found in the Bible. However, as we live life on a day-to-day basis, we understand—sometimes painfully—that there's much more to know about God than we can humanly understand. We come to recognize that we won't have all the answers nor will we fully comprehend the nature of God while we're still on earth. There comes a time when we must live with the unanswered questions and take what Soren Kierkegaard refers to as a "leap of faith."

The beginning of Job provides us with yet another description of God's character that we don't often consider. It shows God involved in a conversation with Satan. Have you ever thought about what God might be doing while you work, sleep, eat, or play? Had you ever pictured God carrying on a conversation with Satan? Through the context of the entire Bible, we can be assured that God and Satan are truly enemies. God is not "kicking back" with Satan while they discuss the merits and challenges of their roles.

What about Satan? The Bible gives us a less detailed profile on Satan's specific actions, but 1 John says much about him:

- He's called "the devil" in 3:8 and the "evil one" in 2:13-14; 3:12; and 5:18-19.

- We know he's been sinning from the very beginning, according to 3:8.

- His origin is not specifically given, but John 8:44 tells us he was not "holding to the truth," which could imply he was a fallen being.

- 1 Timothy 3:6 shows us that Satan was under judgment by God because of his pride.

- Some scholars don't subscribe to the Isaiah 14:12-14 and Ezekiel 28:12-15 passages as applying to Satan, while others believe these clearly show his rebellion before the fall of Adam and Eve.

- Back to 1 John, where it shows that Satan moves humans to sin and all those who sin belong to him (3:8,12), and are even called his children (3:10).

- Satan is a part of the world (1 John 4:3) and "the whole world is under the control of the evil one" (5:19).

- 1 John 5:18 tells us Satan cannot harm believers; they are kept safe by God.

- Finally, we learn that Christians have "overcome the evil one" (1 John 2:13-14) and that "the one who is in you is greater than the one who is in the world" (1 John 4:4).

As you prepare for this session, be aware that Satan is alive and working. His desire is for us to understand neither him nor God. He hopes you won't think about how all this works. He loves it when you're unprepared. Pray for clarity and wisdom as you challenge your students to a greater understanding of our almighty God and Satan, who is under God's control.

THE MAIN IDEA

The Bible is clear: Spiritual forces are at work in our world. God created us, God is in control, and through Christ's sacrifice God won the ultimate victory over sin and death for all time. However, Satan is still roaming around the earth, and it is his desire to take life away from us. Thus, we human beings are somewhere in the middle of it all. This chapter explores the roles of God and Satan in the story of Job. Through our study we'll discover where we fit and how we should live.

FOR STARTERS

Option 1: Have students divide into groups of two to four people. Give each group a different section of the newspaper containing world or local news stories. Allow each group about five minutes to go through their section and tally up the number of articles with positive content and the number of articles with negative content. For each positive or negative article they find, students should be prepared to present their reasons why they categorized it that way.

Option 2: In the large group, have students share about positive and negative events that are happening on a global, national, local, or personal scale, and explain why they categorized each event in either a positive or negative way.

REFLECTION

Offer the following questions as a way to reflect on the previous activity:

- *In general, do there seem to be more negative than positive events in the news or vice versa? Why?*
- *What side of the news does the media prefer to report? Why?*
- *Generally speaking, what would our culture say causes the good and bad events in our lives?*
- *What would Christians say causes the good and bad events in our lives?*

TRANSITION STATEMENT

Say something like—*Life isn't fair. We live in a world where any number of good or bad circumstances may come our way. And there are no guarantees, except God will be with us. What's going on behind the scenes? God loves us and he created us to live forever with him in eternity. Satan roams the earth bringing evil and destruction wherever he goes. And we live in the midst of this battle for our souls. Where do we fit in? Are we like toys that God and Satan just throw back and forth between them? How do we respond?*

Today we begin our study of Job. The book of Job is about a man God loves. This is a man who has been faithful to God throughout his life. Job loves and obeys God, yet he still experiences great suffering. These chapters deal with many of the great questions we ask about the role of pain, disease, unhappiness, loss, and death in our world—all under the compassionate care of our almighty God.

The first part of this book gives us the big picture of what's to come. As we come to understand this opening scene, we'll be better equipped to translate the dialogue in later chapters.

DISCOVER

Ask students to open their Bibles to Job chapter 1.

OPTION 1: MELODRAMA

Begin your study of this passage by presenting the melodrama called **Job's Very Bad Day** (pages 23-26). Recruit your finest actors and actresses to portray the actions and words found in this portion of Scripture. Try your best to use students who enjoy being animated in their actions and responses. Their enthusiasm will help draw your audience into the drama. (Note: The melodrama covers more verses than you'll actually use in today's session.)

OPTION 2: OUTLINE

Divide students into groups of three or four and give each group a sheet of paper and something to write with. Ask the groups to create a summary outline (using bullet points—short and to-the-point truths) of chapter 1, verses 1-12; and chapter 2, verses 1-6.

For example:

- Job is described.
- Satan comes before God.
- Satan and God have a conversation.

Then ask the following discussion questions:

- *What are some of Job's key characteristics as described in this passage?*
- *What do we learn about his family in the first five verses?*
- *Who initiated the interaction between Satan and God? Why is this significant?*
- *Who and what is the subject of their conversation?*
- *What is Satan accusing God of doing in verse 10?*
- *What rules does God give Satan regarding Job?*
- *Who initiates the second conversation between God and Satan in chapter 2, verse 1?*
- *What does Satan claim in Job 2:4-5?*
- *What rule does God give Satan in this circumstance?*

TRANSITION STATEMENT

Say something like—*So, what's going on in our world? Are God and Satan having conversations about us? Are we merely puppets in their hands? In this next exercise we want to go back to a few basic facts about God and Satan to remind us who's really in control.*

TRANSLATION, PLEASE!

Encourage your students, in their same small groups, to complete the worksheet **The Biblical Truth about God and Satan** (page 27). Give your students an appropriate amount of time and then call them back together for a summary discussion using the following questions:

- *What are the big differences between God and Satan?*

- *Why do you think some people would want to believe Satan doesn't exist?*

- *Who's really in control?*

- *Why do you think God allows Satan to have any power at all?*

- *What do these verses show or tell us about the character of God? How about the character of Satan?*

MAKING IT WORK

When students roam the hallways of their schools, hang out with their friends, or even stay home with their families, they're often asked some difficult questions about their faith. This activity is designed to summarize today's session by helping students get practical with their responses.

Have the students use the backs of their **The Biblical Truth about God and Satan** repro sheets and give them five minutes to do the following activity. Say—*In your own words, create two sentences or less that would accurately describe the character of God to someone who's never heard of him or knows very little about him. Do the same to describe Satan.* If there's time, have two or three share their descriptions.

SO WHAT?

This session has likely raised a lot of questions. Given the variety of theological positions on this subject, you may have thought of additional questions to ask or a different direction to take with the session. Feel free to struggle with the subject matter in the context of your church's theology, as you help your students come to conclusions that are faithful to your tradition.

As you close ask the following questions:

> • *Knowing what you know about the role of God and Satan, how should this influence the way you live?*
>
> • *How should it influence how you tell the story of God's love to others?*
>
> • *How does this first part of Job's story help you in your understanding of evil and suffering in our world?*
>
> • *What further questions do you have as a result of this study? (Offer to follow up on these questions in the future.)*
>
> • *What do you think God would say about you to Satan?*

Close in prayer for your group. Pray for faith and trust in the midst of an unfair world where there are often more questions than answers.

JOB'S VERY BAD DAY

A melodrama adapted from portions of Job 1:1–2:12

CAST

Narrator	Sabeans
Job	Fire
God	Chaldeans
Satan	Mighty Wind
Sons of Job (use a sampling)	Servants
Daughters of Job (use a sampling)	Job's Wife
Messenger 1	Eliphaz the Temanite
Messenger 2	Bildad the Shuhite
Messenger 3	Zophar the Naamathite
Messenger 4	Livestock (donkeys, camels, sheep, and oxen)

SETTING

The narrator stands to the side of the stage and is the only speaker during the melodrama. The other characters act out the monologue, following along on their scripts.

ACTION

(Job enters the stage as the reading begins.)

Narrator: In the land of Uz there lives a man named Job. This man is blameless and upright; he fears God and shuns evil. He has seven sons and three daughters. *(The sons and daughters enter the stage)*

He owns 7,000 sheep, 3,000 camels, 500 yoke of oxen, and 500 donkeys. *(The animals enter and make some noise)*

And he has a large number of servants. *(The servants enter and bow humbly)*

Job is the greatest man among all the people of the East. *(Job exits, taking all of his children, livestock, and servants with him)*

(Now God enters the stage, followed by the angels, with Satan bringing up the rear)

Narrator: One day the angels came to present themselves before God, and Satan also came with them.

God said to Satan, "Where have you come from?"
Satan answered, "From roaming through the earth and going back and forth in it."

Then God said to Satan, "Have you considered my servant Job? There is no one on earth like him; he is blameless and upright, a man who fears God and shuns evil."

"Does Job fear God for nothing?" Satan replied. "Have you not put a hedge around him and his household and everything he has? You have blessed the work of his hands, so that his flocks and herds are spread throughout the land. But stretch out your hand and strike everything he has, and he will surely curse you to your face."

God said to Satan, "Very well, then, everything he has is in your hands, but on the man himself, do not lay a finger."

Then Satan went out from God's presence. *(Satan exits, followed by God)*

(Job's sons and daughters enter and stand on one side of the stage)

Narrator: One day Job's sons and daughters were feasting and drinking wine at the oldest brother's house.

(Job enters and stands on the opposite side of the stage from his kids)

Narrator: A messenger came to Job and said, "The oxen were plowing and the donkeys were grazing nearby, and the Sabeans attacked and carried them off. They put the servants to the sword, and I am the only one who has escaped to tell you!"

While he was still speaking, another messenger came and said, "The fire of God fell from the sky and burned up the sheep and the servants, and I am the only one who has escaped to tell you!"

While the second messenger was still speaking, a third messenger came and said, "The Chaldeans formed three raiding parties and swept down on your camels and carried them off. They put the servants to the sword, and I am the only one who has escaped to tell you!"

While the third messenger was still speaking, yet another messenger came and said, "Your sons and daughters were feasting and drinking wine at the oldest brother's house, when suddenly a mighty wind swept in from the desert and struck the four corners of the house. It collapsed on them and they are dead, and I am the only one who has escaped to tell you!"

At this, Job got up and tore his robe and shaved his head. Then he fell to the ground in worship and said: "Naked I came from my mother's womb, and naked I will depart. The Lord gave and the Lord has taken away; may the name of the Lord be praised."

In all this, Job did not sin by charging God with wrongdoing.

(Once again, God enters first, followed by Satan and the angels)

Narrator: On another day the angels came to present themselves before God, and Satan also came with them to present himself before him.

And God said to Satan, "Where have you come from?"

Satan answered, "From roaming through the earth and going back and forth in it."

Then God said to Satan, "Have you considered my servant Job? There is no one on earth like him; he is blameless and upright, a man who fears God and shuns evil. And he still maintains his integrity, though you incited me against him to ruin him without any reason."

"Skin for skin!" Satan replied. "A man will give all he has for his own life. But stretch out your hand and strike his flesh and bones, and he will surely curse you to your face."

God said to Satan, "Very well, then, he is in your hands; but you must spare his life." *(Satan exits, followed by God)*

So Satan went out from the presence of the Lord and afflicted Job with painful sores from the soles of his feet to the top of his head. Then Job took a piece of broken pottery and scraped himself with it as he sat among the ashes.

(Job's wife enters)

Narrator: His wife said to him, "Are you still holding on to your integrity? Curse God and die!"

He replied, "You are talking like a foolish woman. Shall we accept good from God, and not trouble?" *(Job's wife exits, shaking her head in disbelief)*

In all this, Job did not sin in what he said.

(Job's three buddies come walking along, entering the stage on the opposite side from where Job sits)

Narrator: When Job's three friends, Eliphaz the Temanite, Bildad the Shuhite, and Zophar the Naamathite, heard about all the troubles that had come upon him, they set out from their homes and met together by agreement to go and sympathize with him and comfort him. When they saw him from a distance, they could hardly recognize him; they began to weep aloud, and they tore their robes and sprinkled dust on their heads.

THE BIBLICAL TRUTH ABOUT GOD AND SATAN

SATAN

Biblical Reference	What This Says about Satan
Genesis 3:1	
Mark 1:12-13	
John 8:44	
John 12:31	
1 Peter 5:8	
Revelation 12:9	
Revelation 20:10	

GOD

Biblical Reference	What This Says about God
Genesis 1:1	
Genesis 2:7	
Psalm 31:5	
Proverbs 2:6	
John 3:16	
Romans 8:38-39	
Revelation 4:8	

RESPONDING TO LIFE WHEN IT BLINDSIDES US

SESSION 2: JOB 1:13-22; 2:7-10

LEADER PREP

Sitting at a large youth conference, I heard the speaker expound on the subject of trials and temptations. I'd heard these words many times before, but he also reminded the audience that pain is a given in life and not one of us would escape it in some form or another. I remember looking around at the students in our youth ministry and wishing we could somehow shield them from the hardships and grief that surround us. I wondered what pain I would yet experience.

YOU'LL NEED

- a video clip showing some type of natural disaster
- VCR/DVD player
- TV/video projector
- whiteboard and dry erase marker
- copies of **Instant Messengers** (page 37)
- Bibles
- pens or pencils
- copies of **House Call** (page 38)
- copies of **My Worst Day** (page 39)

Less than two weeks after the conference ended, I found out. One of the very students I wanted to protect was diagnosed with an inoperable brain tumor. And within a year she died. I had wanted so badly to believe that if I just took the right precautions, then I might keep life's pain to a minimum. It doesn't always work that way.

Undoubtedly, you've experienced personal pain. As a leader you've likely walked with your students in the midst of their losses and tragedies. We don't know *when* pain will come; we just know *that* it will come. How do you help your students to know God loves them and walks with them—even during the painful times? How do you respond to your own personal pain?

This session won't "feel good," but it may be one of the more helpful and hopeful studies you lead. Your students won't have any difficulty relating to the topic, and some of them will, sadly, know it all too well.

Before the session, find some people who have struggled through great suffering. Interview them to find out how God comforted them, how they overcame the challenge to their faith, and what they ultimately learned. This will give you a fresh context for leading your students through the session. Meditate on Psalm 23 and let Job's attitude of accepting the good and the trouble (Job 2:10) challenge you in your daily life.

THE MAIN IDEA

It's easy to believe that life can be pain-free if we just do the right things. Real life, though, shows us otherwise. In this life pain is guaranteed. We don't know when it will come, but it's inevitable to one degree or another. How should we respond when disease, suffering, loss, or even death unexpectedly comes to us? This session will explore Job's sudden turn of events and how he chose to respond. Through this study your students will discover the meaning of God's sovereignty, as well as what it means to have faith in the midst of trouble.

FOR STARTERS

OPTION 1:

There are many disaster films—old and new—available for rent. Find one and show a five-minute clip of the actual disaster. Most of the special effects in these movies are so artificial, especially in the older films, there is very little graphic violence to worry about.

Here are a few ideas to stir your thinking:

1. *The Day After Tomorrow* (20th Century Fox, 2004)—the storm scene in Los Angeles or the tsunami in New York City

2. *Dante's Peak* (Universal Pictures, 1997)—scenes with lava flowing into the town

3. Other ideas include—

    • Actual footage of tsunami, hurricane, tornado, or earthquake destruction

    • A brief clip of someone who has cancer or another serious illness

The goal is to help students experience, albeit in a very limited way, what it's like to be on the receiving end of an unfortunate turn of events.

OPTION 2:

On a whiteboard, with the help of the group, create a list of all the negative, life-changing events that could happen to a person. Encourage your students to think broadly (i.e., common diseases, storms, robbery, violence, and so on), but at the same time not be too overly specific or graphic (i.e., right leg falling off, left arm falling off, and so on).

REFLECTION

Follow either of the previous activities with these discussion questions:

- *When a disaster strikes, what is typically our first response?*

- *For those of you who've experienced a disaster firsthand, what was your response?*

- *What other responses have you seen among your friends or in the media?*

- *Who commonly gets the blame for almost all disasters? Why?*

TRANSITION STATEMENT

Say something like—*It is inevitable that sometime during our lives we'll experience personal events of a tragic nature. We want to believe these things only happen to other people, but we live in a fallen, sinful world where life includes suffering, loss, tragedy, and death. Throughout the Bible, God reminds us of his constant presence in the good and the bad. How do we respond? How should we respond? Today we'll look at Job's situation and we'll discover how he responded.*

We'll also discover helpful tools we can use in times of our own personal calamities.

DISCOVER

Distribute copies of **Instant Messengers** (page 37) and have students open their Bibles to Job 1:13-22. Invite them to begin working on the sheet either individually or in pairs. Encourage them, if you have room, to find a quiet space to work on this. After a reasonable amount of time (i.e., when most, if not all, of the students are finished) bring the group back together.

Go over **Instant Messengers** and then follow up with these discussion questions:

• *If you were Job, how would you have responded to the first messenger?*

• *Why do you think the Bible doesn't actually tell us how he responded to the first, second, or third messengers?*

• *What was the source of the first tragic event? The second? The third? The fourth?* (1. The Sabeans; 2. Fire of God from heaven; 3. The Chaldeans; 4. The mighty wind)

• *What pattern do you see here?* (earthly, heavenly, earthly, heavenly)

• *Some have said, "Good things come in waves." The same can be said about bad things. Have you experienced this before? Describe.*

• *If you'd never heard this story before, did Job's response to this "wave" of events surprise you? Why or why not?*

• *What was the significance of Job tearing his robe and shaving his head?* (customary ritual of grief in those times)

• *What is Job really saying in verse 21?* (God is in control)

• *What do we learn about Job in verse 22?*

• *Why does God often get blamed for tragedy in our lives?* (Remind students that insurance companies often label storms or earthquakes as "acts of God.")

Following this discussion, have students turn to Job 2:7-10. Give a quick review by reading verses three through six. Then ask one or a few students to read verses seven through ten out loud.

Distribute copies of **House Call** (page 38) and ask students to work in groups of three or four to complete Job's medical assessment. When this is complete, bring the students back together to reflect on the passage with these questions:

• *What's the condition God gives Satan?* (Satan can do whatever he wants to Job, but he must spare his life.)

• *According to verse 7, what do we know about the sores Satan gave Job?* (The Hebrew word for *sores* is actually translated "boils." Without getting overly graphic, you may want to take a moment to describe what it's like to have a boil.)

• *In verse 8 how does Job respond?* (Job was sitting in the junkyard, surrounded by broken things, so he picked up broken pottery to help relieve the itching. Sitting among ashes was the ancient way for expressing one's deepest grief.)

• *What's significant about Job's wife criticizing him in verse 9?* (His potentially biggest encourager became his biggest discourager.)

• *Job calls his wife foolish. What profound statement does he then make? How would you summarize what he's saying?*

• *What's the final statement about Job at the end of verse 10?* (Explain to the students that what a person says is expressive of their deepest thoughts. Job was a man of his word, so it could be accurately translated that he didn't commit even the smallest error in his response.)

TRANSLATION, PLEASE!

These passages paint a disheartening picture of how quickly tragedy, suffering, and even death can come upon us. None of us is immune. Someday, sometime, it will be our turn to respond. How will we do?

Take a quick poll of your group. Ask the students, *How well do you think you'd respond to tragedy in your life? On a scale of one to five, with five being, "I don't think I'd sin at all," and one being, "I'd blame everything on God and not want to follow him any longer," please rate yourself. And be honest.* Create some imaginary sections that correspond to the five different ratings and encourage your students to walk to the section that best fits their response.

MAKING IT WORK

Help students move from Job's story to their own by going through **My Worst Day** (page 39). This is an individual project. Give students an appropriate amount of time to work through their situation and then come back together. If time allows ask a few students to share their answers.

SO WHAT?

In this life we'll experience pain. For some it will be worse than for others, but following Christ doesn't shield any of us from experiencing pain, suffering, or even death. Thus, we, like Job, are forced to decide what our responses will be during those inevitable moments. Often the best preparation for how to respond is walking with others through their pain.

Ask students to either identify or silently pray that God will lead them to one person who needs the comfort of a friend in the midst of a difficult circumstance. Give them a few silent moments to ponder this. If you have time, invite a few students to share about the person they plan to comfort.

Close with a time of prayer for those who are suffering and for those in your group who will be going out to help someone in the midst of pain.

INSTANT MESSENGERS

Read Job 1:13-22 and complete the chart below.

Messenger	When They Came to Job	The Bad News	Job's Response
#1 (vv. 13-15)			
#2 (v. 16)			
#3 (v. 17)			
#4 (vv. 18-19)			

HOUSE CALL

You're a doctor and you're making a home visit to assess Job's physical condition. Based on what's described in the following verses in Job, what do you find?

Verse(s)	Symptom
2:7	
2:12	
7:13-14	
17:7; 19:20	
19:17	
30:17	
30:28,30a	
30:30b	

If you were writing a report for Job's medical file, how would you summarize his condition?

MY WORST DAY

If we believe tragedy only happens to other people, then the story of Job is just a story. But the truth is—we'll all face tragedies to one degree or another. The point of this exercise is to take a look at our own stories and examine either how we responded (if we've already experienced some of life's heartbreaks) or how we predict we'd respond in light of such circumstances.

1. Describe a tragedy that has occurred in your life or describe what you'd consider to be the worst calamity that could happen to you (not including your death).

2. What was your first emotional response (crying, shock, anger)? Or based on your personality, what do you predict might be your first response?

3. Who was most helpful to you in the early moments after you heard the news? Or who do you believe would be the most helpful?

4. What did your helpful friends say or do that comforted you the most? Or what do you believe would be most helpful to you?

5. At the beginning of this difficult experience, what role did you believe God played in it? Or knowing your own relationship with God, how do you predict you'll view him during the early moments of tragedy?

HOW TO BE—AND HOW NOT TO BE—A FRIEND TO THOSE WHO ARE SUFFERING

LEADER PREP

At first glance this appears to be a short study. The passage only covers three verses. However, packed into those three verses you'll find the "seeds" for longer discussion and teaching on the subject of how to help a hurting friend. Almost everyone has experienced those awkward moments of being in the presence of someone who's recently experienced an incredible loss, death, or other tragedy. You may have had the experience of going to visit such a person. On the way there, you may have thought, "What can I possibly say to this person? Does he even want me to be there? Maybe I should turn around and go home. He probably needs his space."

If you've experienced these conflicted feelings before, consider yourself one of the crowd. Many people can relate to those feelings. Even people who've had extensive experience in this arena will often find they're anxious about the interaction to come. Each experience is unique, but we all want to do the right thing.

How do we respond? If we're not careful, it becomes easy to try to "fix" it. We want hurting people to say, "Thanks, I feel better now!" Yet, reality tells us differently. We can never fix a hurting person's situation. Only God can bring healing to those in pain. He may use us as an instrument to do so, but it's ultimately his work.

Read and re-read this passage. Note the intentions of Job's friends. If their roles had ended here, we'd probably have a more favorable view of their part in Job's story. Their desire was to "sympathize with him" (vs. 11) and "comfort him" (vs. 11). Even though they could hardly recognize him, they still approached and sat with him. Note how long they stayed near him without saying a word.

The *ministry of presence* is a phrase used often in ministry circles. It refers to the priority of being more than doing when we're seeking to help another person. Job's friends gave us an amazing example of this ministry with their weeklong stay! While God may not be calling us to spend that long with a person, he is challenging us to think beyond our words.

As you prepare for this lesson, reflect on a time where you "sat" with someone. Who may need your presence now? Pray for your availability to be present with a needy student in the coming weeks.

THE MAIN IDEA

Being a friend to someone who is suffering is never easy. Many people feel awkward; others are so afraid they'll do the wrong thing that they end up doing nothing. In this session and through the study of this passage students will discover positive strategies for supporting their hurting friends, as well as words and actions they should avoid.

FOR STARTERS

OPTION 1:

Give each student a copy of **Bad Words and Other Dumb Things to Do and Say** (page 48) and something to write with. Have students pair off and complete the exercise.

OPTION 2:

Ask students to share about some times when people tried to comfort them and either said unhelpful words or just failed to help in general. Give them some time to think about their own experiences, while you share one of yours.

REFLECTION

Follow up either of the previous options with these questions:

 • *When someone is trying to comfort a hurting person, do you think the comforter's intentions are mostly good or bad? Why?*

- *If their intentions are mostly good, then what goes wrong during their actions?*

- *When you're hurting, how much do comforting words help you?*

- *When you've experienced a tragedy, how can a friend comfort you the most?*

TRANSITION STATEMENT

Say something like—*No one would argue against the fact that in the midst of suffering, we'd much rather be happy. We'd also like everything and everybody to be at peace and whole again. Our friends desire this for us as well; so through their love and compassion, they come alongside to help us.*

In today's passage we find Job at the lowest point of his life. Then, in walk his three friends. In this next activity, we'll discover what Job's friends did right. *Through our discovery we'll learn healthy strategies for helping others and avoiding the unhelpful and sometimes hurtful—yet sadly more common—words and deeds.*

DISCOVER

Ask students to read Job 3:11-13 in their Bibles. Then divide them into smaller groups of three to four and give each group a copy of **Profile of Job's Friends** (page 49) to work through together. Feel free to walk around, answer questions, and encourage the students in their work. After a reasonable amount of time, call everyone back together.

TRANSLATION, PLEASE!

Review the groups' discoveries about these three friends, and list their responses on a whiteboard for all to see. Seeing the responses displayed up front may help the students think more deeply about the men's characteristics and notice parts of the profile they may have missed the first time.

After the group's profile of Job's friends is complete, ask—

- *What brought these three men together?*

- *What was most impressive about them?*

- *Were there any surprises in how they responded to Job? If so, why did that particular response surprise you?*

- *What is it about tragedy that brings friends together?*

- *If we were to stop the session right here, what would you say you've learned about how to respond to a hurting person?*

MAKING IT WORK

Divide your group into two equal teams for a game we'll call "Good Friend/Bad Friend Encore." The object of the game is to be the team with the most points in the end.

Here are the directions:

- Cut apart **Good Friend/Bad Friend Encore** (page 50) along the dotted lines, put the slips of paper into some kind of container, and mix them up.

- Choose two of your leaders to judge the students' comforting responses to their hurting friend. The judges will give points based on the appropriateness and reasonableness of each student's statement. (If you don't have adult leaders, do the judging yourself.)

• Have the teams go to opposite sides of the room. Place a chair in the middle of the room.

• To begin the game, invite one person from Team A to sit in the chair and choose one situation from the container. Give her a moment to silently read the slip of paper and then ask her to describe the situation to the group. She should use her own words and act as though it actually happened to her. Encourage her to be as dramatic as possible and role-play the circumstance.

• After she finishes describing her plight, one person from Team B should approach the hurting person in the chair and offer a short statement of comfort using words that are helpful. This person represents the first "Good Friend."

• Next, invite a person from Team A to act as a second "Good Friend" and provide a new statement of comfort using different helpful words.

• Finally, a second person from Team B should walk over and serve as the "Bad Friend" by trying to comfort the seated person using words that aren't helpful.

• The two leader-judges should score the quality of each response based on appropriateness (encourage students not to be vicious or overly personal with their comments) and reasonableness (statements about aliens, talking animals, killer tomatoes, and so on, aren't considered reasonable), then assign points to the "Good Friends" teams. If the judges agree that a particular statement doesn't fit the criteria, then that person's team must immediately send out someone else to make a new statement, or the team will lose a point.

- At the end of each round, a new person from the opposite team will be chosen to sit in the chair and describe a new situation from the container. Repeat the process until you run out of time or situations.

- Feel free to adapt these rules to your own personal tastes and youth group situation.

SO WHAT?

On a daily basis, we're surrounded by hurting people. Some may be hurting over what might seem to us like trivial matters, while others are feeling the pain of much more significant events. In most cases it's not for us to decide what is or isn't worthy of our time. God has called us to comfort those who need it. As you close this study, it's important to help your group focus more specifically on the hurting people they may see every day, and how they can sympathize with and comfort them.

Ask this question: *Who is one person that God is calling you to care for and comfort?* Give your students a few silent moments to let God help them identify that one person. At the end of the silence, ask them to be honest and raise their hands if they have somebody in mind. If they don't have anyone in mind, ask them to pray for God's direction in leading them to the right people.

Have the students use the backs of their handouts to write down the names of the people to whom God is leading them and the first steps they'll take in being good friends.

Before you dismiss them, lead a prayer of blessing for your students, asking for God's wisdom as they seek to reach out to the people he has identified and the courage to follow through in caring for them.

BAD WORDS AND OTHER DUMB THINGS TO DO AND SAY

Find a partner and create or identify the worst things people might say or do in response to helping a friend in the following situations.

SITUATION 1
Your friend has experienced a death in his family.

SITUATION 2
Your friend has just been diagnosed with a terminal illness.

SITUATION 3
Your friend unexpectedly received a failing grade on a major school project.

SITUATION 4
Your friend's boyfriend (girlfriend) just told her (him) the relationship is over.

SITUATION 5
Your friend was in a serious accident that disfigured her face.

PROFILE OF JOB'S FRIENDS

Job's friends were unique individuals. They came from different backgrounds, looked different physically, and had varying attitudes and responses. Working together in your small groups, discover as much as you can about these men using Job 2:11-13. List their common characteristics. But before you open your Bibles, read the following historical background information about each man, and then copy down the remainder of your discoveries from the passage. You should use all the facts but feel free to read between the lines as well. Use your imagination and have fun!

HISTORICAL BACKGROUND

Eliphaz the Temanite—His name literally means "God is fine gold." He came from the nation descended from Esau. They were well-known for their wisdom.

Bildad the Shuhite—His name most likely means "son of Hadad." (Exciting, huh?) He lived in Shuah. This may have been a tribal place. Shuah was the name of a son born to Abraham by Keturah.

Zophar the Naamathite—His name literally means "young bird." He came from Naamah, an area named after a female descendant of Cain. King Solomon married an Ammonite princess named "Naamah."

GOOD FRIEND/BAD FRIEND ENCORE

Cut along the dotted lines and place these slips into a container for each role player to choose.

You come home from school one afternoon to find your mom and dad sitting in the living room with concerned looks on their faces. They ask you to sit down. They tell you something tragic has happened. Your favorite uncle was killed in a head-on collision.

In the summer before your freshman year of high school, you begin experiencing some strange symptoms. You tell your doctor about it, and he orders some tests. A week later, you find out you have leukemia.

You've been dating a person of the opposite sex for almost a year now. Your relationship is a close one, and you love being with this person. Before first period today, you opened your locker and found a note waiting for you. It said, "It's been great, but I want to date other people now."

As far as you can tell, your parents have been happily married for 25 years now. But in the last month or so, you've noticed they don't kiss or hug each other very often, and they don't really talk to each other either. You can't remember the last time the two of them went out on a date. One Saturday morning your dad invites you to go out to breakfast with him, and he informs you he's seeking a divorce from your mom.

Last night a tornado touched down in your town. It stayed on the ground for only a few minutes, but it hit your house, which is destroyed.

You live in an urban area where gang violence is a constant threat. You hear regular reports about people you know being injured or threatened by gangs. Tonight you're sitting at home when the phone rings. Your mom picks up the phone, says hello, listens for a moment, and then sobs uncontrollably. Your brother has been shot, and he's in critical condition at the local hospital.

THE RELATIONSHIP BETWEEN SIN AND SUFFERING

LEADER PREP

The link between sin and suffering is one that has been in place since Adam and Eve's decision to disobey God's command. In Genesis 3, God pronounced the consequences of their sin. He told them they'd be placed outside the Garden of Eden. He told Eve he would "greatly increase" her pains during childbirth. He told Adam, "Cursed is the ground because of you; through painful toil you will eat of it all the days of your life" (v. 17).

With this account and the many that follow, men and women across the ages have naturally tied their suffering to sin. Throughout the history of the Israelites, we find their disobedience is directly related to diseases, wandering in the wilderness for decades, defeat at the hands of their enemies, and the death of many.

> ### YOU'LL NEED
> - copies of **Is This for Real?** (page 60)
> - pens or pencils
> - copies of **Why Me?** (page 61)

If we think about this logically, we could safely state that because sin is in the world, we must also endure suffering. Almost every form of suffering finds its source in our personal sins, the sins of others, or just sin in general down through the ages. In this context we can explain (though not fully answer) many of our life situations. A few examples illustrate this:

- The person who dies of lung cancer after many years of smoking
- The person who is killed by a drunk driver
- The plane crash caused by mechanical failure (the result of an imperfect human being working on a machine)
- Mudslides in a third world country (the result of greedy people who chose to deforest the land)
- Those with diseases directly related to unsanitary conditions or radiation exposure

These are just a few of the many instances where suffering could be directly related to sin. However, others seem less obvious:

- The young child diagnosed with an inoperable brain tumor
- The baby born with a physical deformity
- The autistic person who must somehow try to live in a functional way

Some might say these are a direct result of the imperfections and limitations we experience as sinful people. They'd be right, but a clear and direct connection just isn't there, which causes these cases, and many more like them, to appear unfair.

In John 9 Jesus confronted this "sin-therefore-suffering" controversy. He came upon a man who was blind from birth.

The disciples asked him, "Rabbi, who sinned, this man or his parents, that he was born blind?"

Jesus answered, "Neither this man nor his parents sinned."

In the *Reflecting God Study Bible*, Kenneth Barker writes, "The disciples were asking an informed question. In those days the rabbis had developed a principle that 'There is no death without sin, and there is no suffering without iniquity.' It is said they even thought a 'child could sin in the womb or that its soul might have sinned in a preexistent state.' They also believed that horrible things happened to certain people because their parents had sinned" (Zondervan, 2000, p.1611).

Jesus said *no* to the disciples and healed the man.

Job's friends come at him with the same understanding as the disciples. Job knows he isn't perfect, yet he's been faithful. He somehow senses that his suffering isn't connected to his sins.

This session will you give you the opportunity to lead your students through the process of understanding how to respond to those circumstances that have no good or reasonable explanation and cause us to ask God the tough questions. Pray for wisdom, discernment, and a listening ear as you walk with your students through this session.

THE MAIN IDEA

Many people believe their suffering is directly related to their sins. This is what Job's friends also believe. Thus, their method for comforting him is trying to explain why he's suffering and pointing out how he must have sinned. Today's study will take a deeper look at this false notion, and students will discover the true relationship between sin and suffering.

FOR STARTERS

OPTION 1:

Help your students understand what it feels like to receive foolish advice. Distribute copies of **Is This for Real?** (page 60) and something to write with. They should work through this quiz individually.

OPTION 2:

As a group, offer students the opportunity to share about a time when they received advice that wasn't true. Ask those who are willing to share to describe the situation, the advice, what type of person gave them this advice, and the consequences.

REFLECTION

(Skip this part if you elect to do Option 2.) Go over the following list of correct answers for **Is This for Real?** and briefly talk about why each answer is true or false.

Correct Answers

1. False *(drink plenty of fluids, eat regularly)*

2. False *(according to the American Red Cross, it isn't necessary; but you should at least let your food start to digest)*

3. False

4. True *(fish is a good source of omega-3 fatty acids)*

5. False *(spicy food may aggravate ulcers, but it doesn't cause them)*

6. False *(they contain Vitamin A and help maintain healthy eyesight, but they don't improve it)*

7. False *(cold weather, wet hair, and chills don't cause colds—viruses do)*

8. False *(it won't do any harm, though your eyes may get more tired)*

9. False *(watching television won't hurt your eyes, though there certainly could be other negative effects)*

10. False

11. False *(tends to cause hand swelling, decreased grip strength, and can result in impairment)*

12. False

13. False

14. True *(just 15 minutes of listening to loud music can cause temporary hearing loss)*

15. True and False *(studies show that no specific food has been proven to cause acne, although some people may notice different reactions after eating certain foods)*

Ask these next questions as a way to summarize either of the latter options:

- *From where do these false advice statements originate? From experience? From somebody's creative mind? Where?*
- *Why do we believe them?*
- *How do we finally learn what is true or false?*

TRANSITION STATEMENT

Say something like—*In the midst of Job's agony and tragic circumstances, his well-meaning friends try their best to fix the problem. They sincerely believe Job must have done something wrong to bring this much tragedy into his life. In their desperation to come up with a reason, they oversimplify the relationship between sin and suffering. Today we're going to study one of the many Scripture passages that refer to this relationship and discover the truth.*

DISCOVER

Begin by having someone read aloud Job 8:1-22—dramatically. The reader could be one of your students (be sure to ask him in advance so he comes prepared), one of your leaders (better ask her ahead of time, too), or yourself. The key is to help students put themselves on the receiving end of Bildad's speech. Remember: He didn't read his thoughts to Job. Instead, he was probably very passionate and intense as he delivered his message. Encourage your reader to present the passage to the group using these same qualities.

After the passage has been dramatically delivered, help your students reflect on it by making the following statement—*Now put yourself in Job's place and give me a few words to describe how you feel after hearing this.*

Have students form groups of four to six people (they can also be smaller or larger than this, depending on your group's size). Ask the groups to imagine they're a small law firm charged with arguing Bildad's point of view. Using Bildad's published speech in Job 8:1-22, challenge each law firm to construct the main points of their case against Job. (They can use the backs of their handouts to make any notes.)

After a reasonable amount of time has passed, allow each group to share one point of their argument until all of Bildad's statements have been covered. With each point that's presented, have students clarify—either through example or some other method—why this statement might be logically true.

TRANSLATION, PLEASE!

On the surface Bildad's argument might seem sound. Assess the perspective of your group by asking the following questions:

- *What is true about Bildad's argument? Why?*
- *What is false about his line of reasoning? Why?*

Leave the students divided into their law firms, but then divide the firms equally, if possible. Have some groups work on question 1, while the others work on question 2:

1) Identify at least two other Bible stories that might reinforce one of Bildad's points. Be ready to explain your reasoning.

2) Identify at least two other Bible stories that might argue against one of Bildad's points. Be ready to explain your reasoning.

After an appropriate length of time, ask the groups to present their findings, alternating between the groups with biblical stories in support of Bildad and those with stories that argue against him.

TRANSITION STATEMENT

Say something like—*Bildad's line of reasoning, though based in some experience, is faulty. When we choose to disobey God, we'll make life more difficult for ourselves, as sin results in negative consequences. However, we've also observed times when we've experienced a tragedy or a time of suffering with no direct relationship to any sin in our lives. Suffering is a result of sin in our world, although our suffering may not always be directly related to our own sins. Now it's time to practice sorting out the relationship between sin and suffering in our own lives and in the lives of others.*

MAKING IT WORK

Have students remain in their "law firms" to complete the next exercise. Distribute copies of **Why Me?** (page 61) to each group. Give them time to read through both case studies and answer the questions that follow.

When they've finished, bring the groups back together and discuss these questions:

- *Why are we so determined that we must fix certain life situations for ourselves or for others?*

- *What's good about this desire? What's bad about it?*

- *After living in some of these difficult situations, what are some practical ways we can either help others or re-alize God's ultimate victory—over sin, suffering, and death—and the hope we can have as a result?*

SO WHAT?

Close today's session by offering these helpful tips (you or your students may want to add others) toward a healthy approach to sin and suffering. Feel free to expound upon and personalize them, if possible:

1) God is in control. Sin has no power over him.

2) God is just. If we've been faithful to him, we will receive an eternal reward.

3) God walks with us through our suffering. He calls us to walk with others and pray for them.

4) Let God be God. Stating some possible reasons why a person is suffering isn't helpful. We aren't the repair person. Let God use you to simply care for your friend.

Finish the session with a prayer for strength and wisdom to put sin and suffering in perspective, and ask God to bless your group by reminding them of the power he'll give them to face adversity with the confidence of his love.

IS THIS FOR REAL?

For each statement below, write the letter T for true or F for false.

1. _____ Feed a cold, starve a fever.

2. _____ Wait an hour after eating before you swim.

3. _____ Coffee stunts your growth.

4. _____ Fish is brain food.

5. _____ Spicy foods can cause ulcers.

6. _____ Eating carrots will improve your eyesight.

7. _____ If you go outside with wet hair, then you'll catch a cold.

8. _____ Reading in dim light will damage your eyes.

9. _____ Too much TV is bad for your eyes.

10. _____ If you cross your eyes, they'll stay that way.

11. _____ Cracking your knuckles causes arthritis.

12. _____ Hair grows back darker or thicker after you shave it.

13. _____ Chewing gum takes seven years to pass through the human digestive system.

14. _____ Too much loud noise can cause hearing loss.

15. _____ Chocolate causes acne.

(Sources: www.kidshealth.org/parent/positive/family/old_wives_tales.html and www.snopes.com/oldwives/oldwives.asp)

WHY ME?

Imagine a client has walked into your law firm, presented one of the following situations to you, and asked you to offer a defense against an opponent who says your client did something to deserve his or her suffering. How will you defend the case?

CASE #1

The young mother of your client has smoked since she was a teenager, and now she's been diagnosed with lung cancer. Your client is only a teenager, and she has two younger siblings. While her dad will still be alive, your client is overwhelmed by a sense of loss and doom. Her mom quit smoking five years ago, turned her life around, and has since been a faithful Christian, wife, and mother. In their desperate attempts to find answers, your client's friends have tried to comfort her by saying this is a natural consequence of her mom's choices and now her mom's sin has brought suffering to others as well. How will you help your client?

What the other side will say:

The truth is:

CASE #2

Recently, there was a massive fire in a crime-ridden urban area near your law firm. The fire destroyed an entire block of apartments. Fire investigators determined the cause to be faulty electrical wiring in one of the dwellings. Two deaths were reported, and all residences were completely destroyed by the quickly moving blaze. In today's newspaper you notice a commentary written by a well-known pastor in the community. He states that perhaps this was God's punishment for the rampant drug abuse, alcoholism, and violence in this community. While you're still reading the article, a potential client walks in—a happily married, young father of three little girls. He shares that his joy is in the Lord, despite the tragic loss of his home and everything he owned. Yet, he's come to you, knowing what this pastor said in the paper, and wonders if he or his family did something that might have brought God's punishment down on them as well. How will you help him?

What the other side will say:

The truth is:

A TEST OF FAITH—PERSONAL, NOT INTELLECTUAL

LEADER PREP

In the course of living our Christian lives, we talk much about faith. The word *faith* is used in the Bible more than 420 times. Hebrews 11 reminds us that "faith is being sure of what we hope for and certain of what we do not see" (v. 1). Faith is essential for our understanding of God. We can know many truths about God, but then there are many we cannot know. It is during those moments that we must have faith.

I once heard a terminally ill person say, "I don't know that there is a God; I don't know if there is a heaven. But I have faith there is a God, and I have faith there is a heaven." This man gives a clear distinction between an intellectual relationship and a faith-filled relationship.

YOU'LL NEED

- Copy of **Faith Things** (page 72)
- whiteboard and dry erase marker
- copies of **Man Versus God** (page 73)
- copies of **Intellectual or Personal?** (page 74)
- pens or pencils

There is also a distinction between an intellectual faith and a personal faith. Intellectual faith is one we can easily teach, encourage, and clarify in other people's lives; but personal faith demands that we apply it in our own lives as well. In the good times we effortlessly have faith in God. In the bad times our faith is put to the test.

There is an old story that illustrates the difference between intellectual faith and personal faith. You may have heard it before, but it's worth repeating:

Many years ago there was a famous stuntman by the name of Jean Francois Gravelot. He called himself "The Great Blondin" because of his fair hair. On June 30, 1859, Blondin, a trained tightrope artist, made his first journey across Niagara Falls. He crossed from the American side to the Canadian side in 20 minutes. On his way over, he dropped an empty bottle tied to a piece of twine to a boat below. The bottle was then filled with water and returned to Blondin, who drank it. After he returned to the American side, he celebrated with a glass of champagne, performed a little dance on the rope, and went again—this time crossing in only eight minutes.

On successive crossings (in the years that followed), Blondin crossed again while riding a bicycle, wearing a pair of stilts, and pushing a wheelbarrow. He even crossed at night. One time he crossed while wearing a blindfold and carrying a heavy sack of blankets.

Reportedly, before one of his crossings, he asked the crowd if they believed he could cross the tightrope while pushing a person in a wheelbarrow. According to the story, one person raised his hand and gave an emphatic "Yes!"

Blondin responded by saying, "Hop in then!" but the man politely declined! This man could have had intellectual faith; but when it affected him personally, he changed his attitude.

As you prepare for this session, take the time to check your own faith. Do you find it easier to talk about faith than to practice it? Let your study of this Job passage confront your true relationship with God. May it dare you to walk more closely with the God of all creation and to be available to let God lead you and your students into a deeper faith to face life during tough times.

THE MAIN IDEA

Faith is one of those churchy words we use when times are good. It seems easy to have faith when life is happy or when we only need to keep our faith on an intellectual level. What happens when the realities of this unjust world collide with our happy existence? This session explores one of Job's many statements regarding his faith and relationship with God. Through the study of these verses, you and your students will be challenged to examine the true meaning of personal faith and how to live it in the best and worst of times.

FOR STARTERS

OPTION 1

Begin this study by having your students form pantomime teams. Cut apart a copy of **Faith Things** (page 72) and divide the slips among the teams so each one has three items to present to the rest of the group. The goal is to get everyone else in the room to identify the situation or thing in which people must put their faith. When the rest of the group has guessed correctly, follow up each item by discussing why faith is required.

OPTION 2:

Invite your group to build a list of all the things and situations in which they must have faith, on a daily basis. Using a whiteboard or some other medium, make a list that all can see.

REFLECTION

Follow either of the latter options with these questions:

> • *Based on your experience with the previous exercise, how would you answer someone who doesn't believe in God and instead says, "I don't have faith in anything"?*
>
> • *How would you define* faith?
>
> • *In what ways do people encourage you to have faith in God? In what ways do people encourage you to have faith in anything?*
>
> • *In what ways do people discourage you from having faith in God? In what ways do people discourage you from having faith in anything?*

TRANSITION STATEMENT

Say something like—*Job's faith in God is deep. In the first session, we discovered the character of Job as being one who is "blameless and upright; he feared God and shunned evil" (Job 1:1). At that point in time, life is happy for Job; he has everything he could ever want and he feels blessed. Some would say it's easy for Job to have faith because God answers his every need. Then tragedy strikes and life changes for Job—his faith is put to the test.*

Today we'll study a passage that's representative of Job's perspective on God during this trying time. He's a man in great pain, and now he feels as though he's in a courtroom with God. He makes statements about God's greatness, but he's also raw in his questioning. Through this session, which only covers a portion of Job's speech, we'll discover how a personal faith works for us in times of trouble.

DISCOVER

Recruit two of your best readers and ask them to read this passage with expression, speaking as they imagine Job would speak. For added effect ask the students to alternate reading the verses: Reader 1 reads the first verse, Reader 2 the second, Reader 1 the third, and so on.

But before they read through the passage, share with the whole group some context for Job's passionate speech. Say something like—*Job's friend, Bildad, has just reminded Job that God cannot be unjust. Therefore, Job and his family must have done something wrong to bring on this enormous amount of suffering. Bildad says Job should ask for mercy and then maybe God will bring him back to full health.*

After the reading is finished, ask your group to summarize what they believe to be Job's point. Your students may come up with a few different answers, and that's good. Your purpose in asking this is to determine if your students are grasping even a small idea of Job's response to Bildad's charges.

Distribute the copies of **Man Versus God** (page 73). Give students the opportunity to form huddles (three to five people, depending on the size of your group) where they can work together on this assignment. The purpose of this exercise is to help students explore Job's shaky-but-personal faith in God during this trying time. Outlining Job's thoughts on the chart will help students see his different views about God and about himself as a representative of all humans.

To give you an idea of how this chart may look, we've provided a partially completed example below:

Verse No.	Thoughts about God	Thoughts about Man
2		How can he be righteous?
3		He could not answer God
4	Wisdom profound, power vast	If we resist him, we could get hurt
5	Moves mountains, overturns them in his anger	
6	Shakes the earth	
7	Speaks to the sun and it does not shine; seals off the light of the stars	
8	Stretches out the heavens; treads on the waves of the sea	
9	Maker of the Bear and Orion, Pleiades, and other constellations	
10	Performs wonders and miracles	
11		I cannot see him; I cannot perceive him
12		If he takes away, I cannot stop him
13	He does not restrain his anger	
14		I can't dispute with him; I cannot argue
15		Even if I were innocent, I could not answer him; I could only plead for mercy

16		He would not give me a hearing
17		Crush me with a storm; multiply my wounds
18		Would not let me regain my breath; overwhelm me with misery
19	In strength he is mighty	In justice what right do I have to call on him?
20		Even in innocence my mouth condemns me. If I were blameless, my mouth would pronounce me guilty

TRANSLATION, PLEASE!

After your students have completed the chart, bring the group back together and begin sorting through their findings with the following reflective questions:

• *What did this exercise teach you about Job's view of God?*

• *What did this exercise teach you about Job's view of himself?*

• *What's Job's bottom line? How would he summarize these first 20 verses in one sentence?*

• *Based on what you've read so far, does Job still have faith in God? Why or why not?*

• *Where does he see himself in relationship to God?*

• *Prior to his tragedies, Job seemed to have a good life and faith in God could have come pretty easily to him. What's the difference between an intellectual faith and a personal faith? Describe the two using examples from Job's situation.*

TRANSITION STATEMENT

Say something like—*Job knew about faith. He even taught his children about it and witnessed to it with his friends. But while his faith was still real during the good times in his life, it was likely an* intellectual *kind of faith.*

After Job experiences a great deal of death—of his children and employees—and destruction, his intellectual faith is put to the test. For perhaps the first time, he must sort out what he really believes about his relationship with God, making his faith more personal *in nature. We get a glimpse of this in Job chapter 19, as we see the raw edges of his interaction with God exposed. In this next section, we'll turn the focus back around to our own lives.*

MAKING IT WORK

In the church or ministry setting, it's very easy for teenagers to give pat or Sunday school answers to real-life problems. Helping them see the difference between how they answer in this context versus how they answer in their unjust world is the objective of this exercise.

Have your students get together in their same huddles; give each group one copy of **Intellectual or Personal?** (page 74) and a pencil or pen. After they've worked through the assignment, invite them to join the larger group and share their work. During each presentation offer quality control input to assure the groups aren't giving stock or easy answers to the real circumstances of life.

SO WHAT?

Summarize the session by helping your students look into their own relationships with Christ. Ask these practical questions:

* *In what areas do you struggle the most to keep your faith personal and strong?*

* *What would help you grow in your faith? (Be real with your answer!)*

* *Who are the friends who walk with you and help keep you strong?*

* *Job knew God was powerful, the Creator of all, and more; yet, he struggled with his limitations and wondered how to relate to his loving and just God. Is your faith big enough to trust God despite the difficult experiences of life?*

As you wrap today's session, there may be students in your group who are confronting a crisis. Encourage students to share their situations with the group, if they feel comfortable doing so. Challenge your group to surround these individuals with their support and care. Close with a prayer for those who've shared their requests, and pray for everyone to keep their faith strong and personal.

FAITH THINGS

Cut along the dotted lines and place these slips in a container so the pantomime teams may each choose one.

Breathing
Flying on an airplane
The sun will not burn up the world

Walking
Driving a car
A person I love will love me back

Hearing
The police won't arrest me without cause (for no good reason)
My brain will help me to think and process

Beating heart
My teacher will give me a fair grade
The ground won't open up and swallow me in an earthquake

Seeing
Doctors and nurses know what they're doing
The food we eat won't make us sick

Tasting
The water we drink won't contain micro-organisms to make us sick
My cell phone will connect me with someone else through a satellite

MAN VERSUS GOD

In Job 19:1-20, Job spells out his relationship with God by describing who Job is, and who Job isn't. In addition, he talks about the character of God. In the chart below, use this passage to outline Job's thoughts about God and his thoughts about humans.

Verse No.	Thoughts about God	Thoughts about Man
2		
3		
4		
5		
6		
7		
8		
9		
10		
11		
12		
13		
14		
15		
16		
17		
18		
19		
20		

INTELLECTUAL OR PERSONAL?

In your small group, create a case study that describes a situation where someone faces a real-life tragedy or crisis. Imagine the person who's experiencing this hard time comes to you for help. He's a Christian, but now he finds himself struggling with his faith. While it's possible to help someone both intellectually and personally, what if you chose to answer him intellectually? What would your response be if you really wanted to help him on a personal level? (It's okay to use an intellectual answer as part of your response.)

The Story…

The Intellectual Response…

The Personal Response…

TALKING TOUGH WITH GOD

LEADER PREP

What would it be like to really talk with God? Have you ever thought about that? Maybe you're saying, "I *do* talk to God." To which I'd say, "Me, too!" But what if God were to respond in a voice that's audible to our ears? What would you say then? How would you say it? What words would you use or not use?

If you grew up in the church, then most likely you were taught how to talk to God. You may have learned from your parents, your pastor, your Sunday school teacher, or other adults. In the process it's likely that you employed some key phrases you'd heard others say. It's possible you even adopted a similar stance or posture. And these words and postures seemed—and may still seem—proper and right.

YOU'LL NEED

• copy of **Let's Play Hardball** (page 84)

• baseball (or other hardball)

• sponge ball (any type will do)

• props for the courtroom scene

• copies of **On Job's Case** (page 85)

• copies of **My Case/My Big Questions** (page 86)

• Bibles

• pens or pencils

In addition, your preferred Bible translation might have had an impact on your prayer style as well. Some people use words such as *thee* and *thou*, while others are fine just saying, "Hey, God!" For every unique human being God created, there's been a distinctive way to converse with the Creator of the universe.

The Bible as a whole does not specifically, in most cases, tell us how to talk to God. Jesus did give us some instructions and a good model for prayer—The Lord's Prayer found in Matthew 6:5-15. In this passage he tells us not to be like the hypocrites and make our prayers a performance. Instead, he suggests we find somewhere private and pray to our Father "unseen." Jesus also tells us not to "babble" like those who believe their many words will impress somebody. Have you ever heard someone pray out loud for 20 minutes straight? Were you impressed?

Then in his model prayer, Jesus gives us all the necessary ingredients of a healthy conversation with God. In John 15:7 he says if we "remain" in him and let his words "remain" in us, then we can "ask whatever you wish, and it will be given you." Yet in both of these cases, as well as other biblical examples, we're not instructed as to *how* we should talk to God.

As we look to some biblical narratives for more clues about prayer, Moses immediately comes to mind. He had an ongoing conversation with God from the time he first meets the God of Abraham, Isaac, and Jacob in that burning bush until his last days on earth, when he looks upon the Promised Land from a distance. Moses understood the power and majesty of God, yet he didn't hesitate to tell God *no* (when God first asked Moses to go before Pharaoh) or to plead with God on behalf of the people who built and worshipped the golden calf in Exodus 32:11.

Job also had a faithful, long-term relationship with God. He freely talked with God and listened to hear his wisdom. In chapter 13 Job wants to argue his case with God. Job knows God is sovereign, but he also has a sense that God actually cares about what Job has to say. In this environment Job feels secure in bringing the facts (as he sees them) to God's attention.

Depending on your tradition or church background, you may have been taught never to question God. While the intent of that teaching was for you to learn to respect and honor God, our study of Job sheds new light on the subject and gives us a different, yet still worshipful, model.

Your students may not have considered the unconditional love and acceptance of a God who welcomes our toughest questions, as well as our doubts. He sees our hearts and knows our true intentions. If we wish to better understand him, love him, obey him, and be faithful, then God wants to walk with us through those uncertainties, just as he walked through them with Job.

What big questions about God, faith, and life are still lingering for you? Bring them before God, and pray about how you might encourage your students to do the same. God created us, God loves us, God is faithful to us, and God will always go with us.

THE MAIN IDEA

We worship God for his majesty, we fear God's mighty power, and we thank him for the gift of life. Our relationship with God is to be one of highest praise, unwavering faith, and respect. In this relationship, though, it's easy to treat God like a distant authority figure who may love us, but only speaks to us occasionally and rarely takes our perspective into consideration when he does. This study focuses on Job's courageous faith before God to speak openly and honestly about his tragic life. In the course of the session, students will discover, through Job's example, the value of an authentic relationship with a loving Father who listens to our greatest joys and our deepest hurts.

FOR STARTERS

OPTION 1

Begin this session with an exercise called "Let's Play Hardball." Arrange a circle of chairs and have everyone take a seat. If you have a large group, you may want to consider forming more than one circle and assigning one facilitator to each group.

You will serve as a facilitator during this exercise. Read aloud the first situation on **Let's Play Hardball** (page 84), then toss the baseball to someone in the circle. The person who catches the ball should respond in a tough, aggressive manner. (An example is offered on the repro page.) After receiving the "hardball answer," the facilitator tosses a sponge ball to a different person in the circle, and they should respond in a more diplomatic, friendly manner. Following this second response, the facilitator reads the next situation on the handout, after which the person holding the baseball tosses it to another person in the circle. Likewise, the person with the sponge ball will toss her ball to a new person once the new hardball person has spoken. This pattern will continue until all the situations have been read.

OPTION 2:

Invite your students to share examples of situations when people tend to talk the most openly, honestly, and sometimes harshly with each other. Also invite students to offer examples of situations when people tend not to speak the truth because they're just trying to be nice, or they're afraid they might offend someone.

REFLECTION

Follow either option with these reflective questions:

- *Is it better to be brutally honest or to be nice without really addressing the problem? Why?*

- *What seems to be the tendency of most people?*

- *Which of these two responses brings the best results, in your opinion?*

- *What is the short-term result of playing "hardball"? What are the possibilities for long-term results?*

- *What's the short-term result of playing "softball"? What are the possible long-term results?*

TRANSITION STATEMENT

Say something like—*Depending upon our personalities, we may find it easy or difficult to be open and honest with ourselves and with others. For many years Job had faithfully followed God, loved his family, and served his community. Everything was nice. When the suffering came, Job's nice life came to a halt. His friends believed Job must have sinned and God was now disciplining him. While Job knew he wasn't perfect, he also knew the circumstances of his present life weren't fair. In chapter 13 we find a clear example of Job's open and honest relationship before God. Through this session we'll discover the value of an authentic relationship with a loving and just God who listens to our greatest joys and our deepest hurts. We'll also discover it's okay to bring our questions and doubts to God.*

DISCOVER

Using a few standard props—which you can probably find in your youth room, church, or home—take the time to create a simulated courtroom. The judge can sit in a chair behind a small table at center stage. To the right of the judge's seat, place three chairs facing the audience. The three friends will sit here. To the left of the judge, place one chair for Job.

Recruit students to play the judge, Job's three friends, and Job. Choose a student with excellent reading skills to play the part of Job, and encourage this person to read the entire passage (Job 13:1-27) with extra feeling and passion. Invite the judge and three friends to respond nonverbally to Job's speech, but with appropriate facial expressions.

When this reading is complete, give the courtroom your thanks and instruct the students to form smaller jury panels (you may determine how many students in each group). Distribute copies of **On Job's Case** (page 85) and direct the jury panels to complete their work as a group, selecting one person to serve as the jury foreman and present their findings when they're finished.

After you've given the jury panels sufficient time to work, reassemble everyone and let each group's foreman share a brief report.

TRANSLATION, PLEASE!

Use the following questions for reflection on Job's case:

- *Do you feel Job was right to play "hardball" with God?*

- *Have you ever talked this way with God?* (Invite any willing student to give an example.)

- *Have you ever wanted to talk this way with God but didn't? What held you back?*

- *As Job is talking tough with God, which of God's characteristics is Job probably aware of?* (His sovereignty and holiness)

- *Does talking with God in this manner cause him to hear us better? Does "hardball" work with God?*

- *What's the effect on us?*

TRANSITION STATEMENT

Say something like—*In the midst of incredible pain, Job shared his honest feelings with God, yet still acknowledged God's power and holiness (see verse 16, "no godless man would dare to come before him"). We worship a God who created us, is in charge, and knows what's best for us. We also serve a God who desires relationship. A relationship requires communication; and in our relationship with God, he expects us to both listen and speak. Given Job's example during this very difficult time, how do we apply this to our own lives?*

MAKING IT WORK

Instruct students to gather into their jury panels (small groups) one more time. Direct each person to write a short description of an unfair life situation (death, broken relationship, loss of property, and so on) on a small piece of scrap paper, fold the paper in half, and drop it into a container of some kind. When everyone in the group has finished, one person should shuffle the situations and walk around the circle, allowing each person to draw out a piece of paper. Using the example of Job, who talked honestly with God and acknowledged God's greatness, let each group member respond to their selected situation with their own response to God. Suggest they use one of the following open-ended statements to get started:

1) "God, I acknowledge you are—"

2) "God, what I don't like about this situation is—"

3) "God, my request is—"

After each group member has had an opportunity to respond, call the group back together.

SO WHAT?

Close today's session by encouraging your students to consider arguing their own cases before God. If they were to appear in God's courtroom, what evidence and arguments would they present? Finish with the exercise found in **My Case/My Big Questions** (page 86).

Following the completion of this page, challenge your students to talk more honestly with God about their circumstances or questions and let him be God in the midst of their pain, injustice, and suffering.

If there's time, invite students to share about a few of the painful situations they're encountering and the questions they listed. Perhaps you could offer a special time during another meeting for a question-and-answer forum. Students could write down their big questions on pieces of paper or index cards. These could be shuffled and addressed individually, giving students and leaders the opportunity to talk through the answers.

End with a time of group prayer for these circumstances and questions. Ask for God's wisdom and guidance in all the situations represented.

LET'S PLAY HARDBALL

SITUATIONS

1. Your teacher gave you a B on a paper, but you believe you deserved an A.

2. You're buying your first car at a used car lot. The salesperson is trying to sell you a vehicle for $500 more than the fair price.

3. You've been hired to wait tables at a restaurant. Your boss wants you to work both Friday and Saturday nights on a consistent basis. You'd like to have at least one weekend night free.

4. Your parents believe you should do more chores around the house. You believe you should be doing fewer.

5. It's your opinion that your closest friend is about to make a bad decision.

6. You're skateboarding in a public parking lot, when a man approaches you and claims you dented his hubcap with your skateboard. You know you didn't do it.

7. Your mom and dad have recently divorced, but they still live in the same town. Your mom wants you to spend time with her on the weekends and with your dad on weekdays. You'd rather do the opposite.

8. The person sitting next to you in third period English has annoying habits that are a real distraction. One day you can no longer let it slide. The time has come to say something.

9. A close friend borrowed your camera for a weekend and brought it back in poor condition. You didn't say anything at the time and took it in for repairs. Now your friend asks to borrow the camera again.

10. You've been having a conversation with a friend about the importance of attending church and participating in the fellowship of other believers. Your friend believes you can still be a Christian without ever belonging to a church.

ON JOB'S CASE

In your jury panel, look through Job 13:1-27 and assess the strength of Job's case before God by completing the following evaluation.

Job's qualifications (what he says positively about himself)

Job's three friends' disqualifications (what he says negatively about his friends)

What we know about the Judge (God)

Job's requests before God the Judge

Job's questions to God

ASSESSMENT

Based on what you've read in this passage, how would you rate the strength of Job's case on a scale of 1 to 5 (1 = weak; 5 = strong)? Explain your rating.

What is Job's strategy with his case? Is he playing it safe or is he daring? How would you rate him on a scale of 1 to 5 (1 = safe; 5 = daring)? Explain your rating.

MY CASE/MY BIG QUESTIONS

Job was ready to argue his case before God. He had many questions, and he was feeling the weight of injustice. Job felt he had a strong argument for why he didn't deserve his recent round of personal tragedies.

If you were allowed to appear in a courtroom before God, what case would you plead? Would you represent a seriously ill friend? Would you represent a friend who has a horrible home life? Would you represent yourself and the injustices or hard circumstances that have come your way recently? Would it be something else?

Explain your point-by-point case below.

•

•

•

•

•

•

You may also have some big questions for God—questions about faith, life, relationships, and more. But let's move beyond questions such as, "Did Adam and Eve have belly buttons?" or "What's the purpose of a housefly, anyway?" Try to think of some more thoughtful inquiries, and write your questions below.

1)

2)

3)

4)

5)

6)

WEIGHING THE WISDOM OF WELL-MEANING FRIENDS
SESSION 7: JOB 16:1-5

LEADER PREP

Have you ever been around someone who seems to know "everything"? You may have heard these people referred to as "A-to-Z"s because they know something about everything, and they don't hesitate to offer their great wealth of knowledge—even in the most inappropriate moments. If you frequently spend time with such a person, then you might consider yourself in competition with him, even trying to come up with a subject or fact about which the know-it-all person knows nothing or very little. Too often, though, you'll have to backpedal when he displays his expertise in the chosen subject matter once again. And so the endless cycle goes.

In the midst of our broken lives and sinful natures, God still maintains our human need to see life situations made whole. While our intentions are respectable, our desires can easily override what's reasonable and we may lack the sensitivity necessary whenever we reach out to real people with real feelings.

Generally speaking, it seems men are particularly prone to try to "fix" things. Physically, the fix-it skill is often handed down, in some form or another, through the generations. Some men pick up these skills more easily than others do, but quite often in a family it's Dad who gets the broken things to repair at his leisure. So it's not surprising that this propensity tends to appear in broken relationships as well, particularly marriages. It's very easy for a husband to suggest a quick "patch up," for example, when what his wife really wants is to be heard and understood.

There are several Bible stories about people who try to fix either things or life circumstances. In Numbers 20:1-13 we read the account of Moses and his bad choice concerning water. The people gather in front of Moses and quarrel with him because there's no water supply available to the community. They even exclaim it would be better to live in Egypt than experience this drought. So Moses and Aaron do what they'd often done before—they go to God for help. When the glory of the Lord appears among them, he tells them to take the staff and gather all the people together. God then tells them to "speak to that rock before their eyes and it will pour out its water. You will bring water out of the rock for the community so they and their livestock can drink" (20:8).

Moses takes the staff, and then he and Aaron stand before the gathered people of Israel. After he asks the question, "Must we bring you water out of this rock?" Moses raises his arm and strikes the rock twice with his staff. The Bible tells us, "Water gushed out, and the community and their livestock drank" (20:11).

This passage is not clear about Moses' motivation for using the staff instead of just his words, as God instructed him to do, but it's pretty clear that he decided his way was better than God's way. And Moses' poor choice cost him dearly. God said to him, "Because you did not trust in me enough to honor me as holy in the sight of the Israelites, you will not bring this community into the land I give them" (20:12).

The lesson is clear: God is God, and we are not. As we serve him in humbleness and understand our role, we will be used most effectively. Job's friends were not ready to heed this message. In today's session we see just one example of their need to fix Job's situation, rather than listen to him and seek to understand.

As you prepare for this session, evaluate your own response to shattered situations. What is your first reaction? May it be one of first calling on God for wisdom and then respectfully following God in obedience.

THE MAIN IDEA

In times of great trouble, friends long to comfort each other. Their good intentions, as in the case of Job's friends trying to help him, can easily be more discouraging than encouraging. In this chapter your students will have the opportunity to explore Job's response to the advice of his friends, how to be a good friend in tough times, and how to assess the wisdom you receive from people who seemingly care.

FOR STARTERS

OPTION 1:

Begin this session with a melodrama called "Mr. Fix-It," based on the widely circulated story of an insurance claim filed by an injured man. Make copies of **Mr. Fix-It** (pages 95-96) and recruit the appropriate number of students for the parts. Though this melodrama could potentially require many props, it will be more humorous and effective if the audience members have to use their imaginations. Some cues have been written into the script, but add as much as you want. Be creative!

OPTION 2:

If your group is less than dramatic, then share a story about a time when you tried to fix something but made the situation worse (the object or situation was destroyed even more) through your own stubbornness. Ask students if they have any "repairs-gone-wrong" stories to share.

REFLECTION

Follow either option with these reflective questions:

- *What feels so good about fixing something?*
- *What is positive about our desire to fix something or to help someone feel better?*
- *What can be negative about this same desire?*

TRANSITION STATEMENT

Say something like—*Many experts seem to believe that males, in particular, care more about fixing things and situations than females do. Females often report they don't want their problems fixed; they just want to be heard. While this may in fact be truer of guys, the reality is that* all *of us desire—on some level—to see something made better. We generally don't like broken things or painful circumstances. So we search for explanations and comforting words to help our hurting friends and relatives cope. Today we'll look at five verses in Job that offer a glimpse of Job's frustration with his friends who, though they seemed to have good intentions, really didn't help him in the end.*

DISCOVER

Have your students open their Bibles to Job 16:1-5. Ask five people who like to read in front of a group to come forward. Have them form a line, standing shoulder-to-shoulder. Beginning from left to right, invite each of them to read—with feeling—one verse.

After the readers are once again seated, follow up with a quick survey of your group. You may want to record their responses on a whiteboard for all to see. Poll them with these statements and questions:

• *Job calls his friends "miserable comforters." In our sessions on Job so far, what do we know about these three guys that would lead Job to characterize them in this way?*

• *When you hear the words* miserable comforters, *what other characteristics come to mind?*

• *Job calls their speeches "long-winded" (also translated*

as "empty notions" in Job 15:2). What did these friends keep saying in their long-winded speeches?

• *What do other miserable comforters you know tend to say in their long-winded speeches?*

• *Job says he could speak like them. How does he describe what they're doing in verse 4?*

• *What other things do well-intentioned friends do or say that don't really help?*

TRANSLATION, PLEASE!

Job states in verse 5 that instead of making long-winded speeches and shaking his head, he'd use his lips to encourage and offer comfort to his friend in need.

Throughout the Bible there are many useful verses to further equip your students in their desire to comfort and be comforted. Help your students turn their attention toward healthy strategies for giving comfort and learning how to gracefully receive both helpful and hurtful (though well-intentioned) words and acts from caring friends. Distribute **Helpful Friends** (page 97), and ask students to form small teams to work together on this project. When the teams are finished, bring everyone back together and wrap up this section by going over these summary questions:

• *What's one important characteristic of a helpful friend that you discovered in your group?* (Have each group share one characteristic.)

• *How would these things bring relief to you or your hurting friend?*

MAKING IT WORK

It's easy for us to teach students how to be helpful; but what happens when we're faced with the reality of helping a suffering person we know well, a little, or not at all?

Ask students to get back into their teams and identify a real-life situation where somebody is suffering. The situation might involve a member of their group, somebody one of the group members knows, somebody at school whom the group members know a little or not at all, a sponsored child in a developing country, or a person they met during a mission trip. You may need to walk around and help each group identify their person in need.

Now distribute copies of **Frontline Friend** (page 98), one to each group. Give them an appropriate block of time to complete the task and then come back together.

SO WHAT?

Hopefully that last activity motivated your students to think about both sides (the giving and receiving ends) when trying to be a friend to somebody in pain. Spend these last few moments reminding them how God desires to use us as a vessel of his love in the lives of those who hurt, but that it's ultimately God who comforts and brings peace and wholeness to a person. We're merely his servants.

Encourage them with these simple tips (you may wish to add your own as well):

1. First, and most importantly, *pray* both for your friend and for your own wisdom.

2. Go and be with your friend. Your presence, whether or not you say a word, will be so important.

3. Listen first and speak second. Don't be too quick to offer advice.

4. Remember you really don't know how another person feels; you can only imagine. Disciplining yourself to say, "I can only imagine..." is helpful. However, sharing about a similar experience of your own probably won't help much, as every situation is different.

5. Express your care and love for your friend. Let him know you're available to help him.

Finish this time with prayer for your group as they go out into their world to love and care for those who are hurting.

MR. FIX-IT

(Adapted from a widely used Internet story, author unknown)

CHARACTERS

Narrator
Injured man
Man who will be injured (also known as "Victim")

PROPS (ALL PLAYED BY PEOPLE)

Bricks (two to four people)
Barrel
Rope
Pulley
First floor*
Second floor*
Third floor*

Represent the building from a horizontal perspective.

Narrator: The following letter comes from a man who was injured on the job. *(Injured man exhibits his injuries.)* Following the injury, he filed an insurance claim. *(Injured man sits down to fill out his claim form.)* But the insurance company needed more information and asked for further explanation. This is the man's letter of explanation. *(Injured man begins writing.)*

Narrator: Dear Sirs:
I am writing in response to your request concerning clarification of the information I supplied in block 11 on the insurance form, which asked for the cause of the injury. I answered, "Trying to fix it myself." I trust the following explanation will satisfy you.

I am a bricklayer by trade. *(The man who will be injured, hereafter referred to as "Victim," pretends to lay bricks.)* On the date of the injury, I was working alone, laying brick around the top of a three-story building. When I finished the job, I had about 500 pounds of bricks left over. *(Victim pretends to lift that amount of bricks.)* Rather than carry the bricks down by hand, I decided to put them in a barrel *(person playing the barrel suddenly appears and is filled with bricks)* and lower them by a pulley that was fastened to the top of the building.

I secured the end of the rope at ground level *(Victim climbs down and secures rope)*, went back up to the top of the building, loaded the bricks into the barrel, and pushed it over the side. I then went down to the ground and untied the rope, holding it securely to insure the slow descent of the barrel. If you look in block 16 of the insurance claim, you'll see I weigh 145 pounds. *(Victim shows pride in his or her figure.)*

At the shock of being jerked off the ground so swiftly by the 500 pounds of bricks in the barrel, I lost my presence of mind and forgot to let go of the rope.

Between the second and third floors, I met the barrel. This accounts for the bruises and lacerations on my upper body. *(Victim displays his or her injuries.)* Fortunately, I retained enough presence of mind to maintain my tight hold on the rope and proceeded rapidly up the side of the building, not stopping until my right hand was jammed in the pulley. This accounts for my broken thumb (see block 4). Despite the pain, I continued to hold tightly to the rope. Unfortunately, at approximately the same time, the barrel hit the ground and the bottom fell out of the barrel. *(Bricks fall out.)* Without the weight of the bricks, the barrel now weighed about 50 pounds. Look again at block 6, where my weight is listed. At this time I began to go back down—and quite rapidly!

In the area of the second floor, I met the barrel coming up. This explains the injury to my legs and lower body. Slowed only slightly, I continued my descent until I finally landed on the pile of bricks. Fortunately, my back was only sprained. I am sorry to report, however, that at this point I again lost my presence of mind—and let go of the rope.

I trust this answers your concerns. Please note that I am finished with trying to fix things myself.

HELPFUL FRIENDS

In your small group, take some time to discover what these passages say about being a helpful friend. The following chart will assist you in this exploration.

Scripture Passage	The Role of a Friend, according to Selected Bible Verses
Proverbs 17:17	
Proverbs 18:24	
Proverbs 19:20	
Proverbs 27:9	
Proverbs 27:17	
Ecclesiastes 4:10	
John 15:13	
Romans 12:10	
Romans 15:7	
Ephesians 4:2	
Ephesians 4:32	
1 Thessalonians 5:11	
1 John 4:7	

FRONTLINE FRIEND

Describe your suffering friend's situation:

Using a helpful friend's characteristics as they're described in the Bible (see **Helpful Friends** on page 72), identify two or three traits you might use to bring comfort and relief in this particular situation. Describe how you'd communicate, what you'd say, how you'd position yourself, where you'd meet, and so on. What might be the realistic response of the person you help?

1) Characteristic: _____

Communication:

Response:

2) Characteristic: _____

Communication:

Response:

3) Characteristic: _____

Communication:

Response:

Now put yourself in the place of a friend who's receiving help. What if the advice, comfort, or relief isn't helpful? Or what if your friend's response seems wrong in your situation? What do you do?

How would God want you to respond?

How is God's wisdom helpful in this circumstance?

WHEN JOY ISN'T HAPPINESS
SESSION 8: JOB 19:1-27

LEADER PREP

I remember the first time I read it: "Let us fix our eyes on Jesus, the author and perfecter of our faith, who for the *joy* set before him endured the *cross*, scorning its shame, and sat down at the right hand of the throne of God" (Hebrews 12:2, emphasis mine). How could this be? How could Jesus be happy about facing torture, ridicule, and ultimately death? I know he was God, but it still doesn't make sense. If Jesus was happy about this, then I had no right to ever be sad. It didn't seem consistent with what I felt or what I'd studied in the rest of the Bible. Jesus was sad about Lazarus' death; and in the garden, just prior to his arrest in Luke 22, he was sorrowful to the point of sweating drops of blood. (Now that's sadness!) How do we reconcile this? Was Jesus capable of two emotions at the same time? Was he in denial about what was going to happen?

YOU'LL NEED

- copies of **The Happy Page** (page 108)

- pens or pencils

- old magazines

- scissors

- paper

- glue

- Bibles

- copies of the **Happy/Sad Chart** (page 109)

- whiteboard and dry erase marker

To know the answer, we must first discover the difference between *happiness* and *joy*. Frequently these two words are used as one and the same. And while they do share some characteristics, they're actually different. Your understanding of this will be helpful as you lead and guide your students through this session.

Happy is defined as, "delighted, pleased, or glad, as over a particular thing." Usually, the emotion of happiness is related to happenings. We can all feel happy over a variety of things: a good meal, loving friends, winning a prize, going on a great vacation, getting a new appliance, car, or electronic device; and more. So when the circumstances are good, we feel happy. When things break, get old, disappoint us, or don't happen the way we want, we feel sad. When we aren't happy, we work to fill that void by buying a new thing, trying a new situation, meeting a new person, or any number of other behaviors that won't satisfy us long term. If we're a normal (i.e., emotionally, physically, and socially healthy) person, then it wouldn't be our desire to remain sad. But some people seem to be sad by design. They have some motivation not to display happiness. It could be said that these people are "happy" to be sad.

On the other hand, *joy*, in the biblical context, is not an emotion, although Webster's dictionary defines it as a "feeling or state of great delight or happiness; keen pleasure; elation." While *joy* is often equated with *happiness* in the human context, it is not synonymous with *happiness* throughout the story of God's people. The word *joy* is found 242 times in the Bible. The word *rejoice* is found another 156 times. Joy is an attitude of the heart. It is not necessarily based on something positive happening.

James 1:2 challenges us to "consider it pure joy, my brothers, whenever you face trials of many kinds." Would anyone believe this could be accomplished if we were talking about happiness as we know it? How could we be realistically happy about trials and hard times? If this is what we had to teach, then finding people to follow Jesus would be difficult at best.

In Philippians 4:4 Paul challenges us to "rejoice in the Lord always. I will say it again: Rejoice!" If Paul was telling us to be happy all the time, we'd find that hard to believe. It might remind us of some televangelist who wants us to send him money so we can always be happy. We wouldn't consider this logical or workable in our lives. Joy is based on the foundation of our hope in Christ. Joy is seeing the light at the end of what may appear to be a long, dark tunnel. Joy is what held Job's faith intact during his darkest hours.

How are you doing at living a joy-filled life? Let the words of Habakkuk inspire you as you prepare your heart and mind for this session: "Though the fig tree does not bud and there are no grapes on the vines, though the olive crop fails and the fields produce no food, though there are no sheep in the pen and no cattle in the stall, yet I will rejoice in the Lord, I will be joyful in God my Savior" (Habakkuk 3:17-18).

THE MAIN IDEA

In this chapter we'll discover a clear definition of how joy is different than happiness and how one can have joy in the midst of sadness.

FOR STARTERS

OPTION 1:

Give all students a copy of **The Happy Page** (page 108) and ask them to complete it on their own. You could add a little atmosphere by playing a recording of some song that includes the word *happy* in its lyrics. Be creative.

When most students are finished, have them find three to five others to join them in a small group (unless you already have a pretty small youth group!). Ask them to share their top five items with each other and give a reason for including them on the list.

After most of the groups have worked through the handout, have them come back together as one large group.

OPTION 2:

Use the old standby activity that includes a pile of used magazines, paper, scissors, and glue. Ask students to grab a magazine or two and work individually to create a montage of pictures. They should either cut or tear out five to 10 pictures of things that make people happy and then glue those pictures onto a sheet of paper. When everyone has completed their work, have them come back together and ask several, if not all, students to share their creations.

REFLECTION

As an effective follow-up to either of these activities, pose the following questions:

- *What would you guess to be the top three things that make most people happy?*

- *How would you describe* happiness *to someone who's never heard the word before?*

- *How do most people look when they feel happy?*

- *Why is happiness so important?*

- *Why is it so difficult to stay happy?*

At the close of this discussion, say something like—*We all want to be happy. So when we aren't, we'll do whatever it takes to find happiness. Job wanted to be happy, but there was nothing in his present life situation that would have offered him true happiness. However, in this chapter we find what appears to be a happy statement! How can that be? Let's look at chapter 19 and discover why.*

DISCOVER

Ask students to open their Bibles to Job 19, but first share this quick bit of background information—*Bildad, as you know, is one of Job's three friends. He believes God is a just God, which is correct. He also believes that because God is just, he won't punish a just person, which is incorrect. Since Bildad believes Job is being punished, he also believes Job must have done something wrong. Like Eliphaz, Bildad believes people suffer as a result of their sins. Bildad's words to Job are often harsh. He even says Job's children died because of Job's sins. That's when Job decides to respond, and that's where we pick up the story.*

Read Job 19:1-27 and complete the **Happy/Sad Chart** (page 109). This may be done as a large group or after breaking up into smaller groups. The point of this exercise is to discover that Job's life story is overwhelmingly tragic and full of sadness. Yet, in the midst of this, he makes a few statements that could be categorized as happy.

Help your students feel the tension by discussing the following questions after the activity:

- *How many happy statements did you find? How many sad statements did you find?*

- *Why could Job make any happy statements at all?*

- *Do you think he was actually happy in verses 25-27? Why or why not?*

- *Is it normal to be happy in the midst of tragedy? Is it possible? How?*

TRANSLATION, PLEASE!

The preceding activity and questions probably raised more questions for your students. In this section you'll guide them toward finding some deeper meaning in this dilemma.

Read James 1:2, then say something like this—*The writer of James encourages us to view times of trouble as being opportunities for joy. If you read that verse again and replace the word* joy *with* happiness, *it doesn't make sense. What's the difference between joy and happiness?*

Using a whiteboard so all can see, you may want to draw a small, two-column chart with the word JOY at the top of one column and the word HAPPINESS at the top of the other. Your purpose is to show the primary difference between *joy* and *happiness*: joy is an attitude; happiness is a fleeting emotion that comes and goes. Joy is something we can have in all circumstances, as it allows us to see that God is still in charge and we can have hope in him. Paul tells us in Philippians 4:4 (NLT), "Always be full of joy in the Lord."

MAKING IT WORK

Use the following case studies to help students identify and implement the proper responses in these challenging situations.

CASE STUDY 1

Chad is one of your close friends. You've known him since kindergarten. Chad's older sister, at the age of 21, recently died from complications related to cystic fibrosis. Chad loved his sister very much, and he's overwhelmed with grief from the loss. Ask students to consider the following responses, decide whether each would be helpful or hurtful, and then explain why. Then they should choose the statement that best reflects an appropriate response in light of what they've learned in Job 19.

- "It must have been her time to go."

- "God needed your sister in heaven."

- "I hurt with you, and I know God wants to walk with you through this difficult time. I am here for you."

- "I am so sorry for what happened to your sister, but it must have been God's plan to take her now."

CASE STUDY 2

Trina is one of your classmates. You know her and talk to her occasionally but mostly about issues related to class-work. During the time you've known her, you've observed she's generally negative about life. You begin by asking Trina about her family and life, only to discover that everything seems fairly normal. You realize Trina's negative attitude has alienated her from many people, and you're one of the few people she interacts with on a regular basis. Perhaps Trina is feeling genuine pain over a particular situation. It's difficult for you to know. How could you help Trina to find joy in her life without saying, "Just get over it"?

CASE STUDY 3

Lito's family lives in a small, two-bedroom house in your community. His mom and dad are hardworking people, and you regularly see them at church. You know Lito's parents are involved in church leadership, attend Bible study, and faithfully serve the church in the community. Recently, a wildfire broke out in a nearby canyon. Before the fire-fighters could stop it, the fire destroyed four homes in your neighborhood, including Lito's. Thankfully, nobody was killed or injured. Your church has surrounded Lito's family and helped them in every way possible.

One night during your small group meeting, Lito explains how he's struggling. On the afternoon when the fire began, Lito and his family had prayed for their own protection and the protection of their home. Instead, the fire raced through the four smallest and oldest homes in the neighborhood and left the mansions intact. Lito says, "I don't understand why God would protect those people. They don't love him. They worship their things. It's not fair! I know God loves us, but he has a funny way of showing it."

How do you respond? Using Job 19, how could you help Lito experience joy in the midst of an unjust and tragic situation? What responses would be helpful? What responses would probably make things worse?

SO WHAT?

Close today's session by challenging students to take what they've learned beyond case studies and good ideas. The attitude of having joy in the Lord is foundational to our survival in this unjust and fallen world.

Have students gather with one or two other people and answer the following questions:

> • *In what area of your life is it or would it be most difficult for you to experience joy?*
>
> • *Who is one person (you don't have to name him) to whom you could bring the joy of the Lord? What will be your first step in doing so?*

Ask the groups to end the time by praying for each other in these specific areas.

THE HAPPY PAGE

What makes you happy? Below, you have an opportunity to create a list of the top 10 things in life that make you smile and explain why. Please list things other than the typical Sunday school answers of God, Jesus, the Bible, and so on. We'll just assume one or more of those make your list!

Top 10 Happy List   **Why?**

1. _____   _____

2. _____   _____

3. _____   _____

4. _____   _____

5. _____   _____

6. _____   _____

7. _____   _____

8. _____   _____

9. _____   _____

10. _____   _____

HAPPY/SAD CHART

Read Job 19:1-27 and complete the chart below. Find all the sad and happy statements contained in this passage and list the verse number where you found each.

Sad Statements	Verse	Happy Statements	Verse

WHY DON'T THE WICKED SUFFER?

LEADER PREP

Why do the good suffer while the wicked go on their merry way? Why does a sweet fifteen-year-old girl die of an inoperable brain tumor? Why does a poor church get destroyed by a tornado? If God loves us so much, why doesn't he protect us more from tragedy?

In your lifetime you may have heard these questions before—and many more like them. You may have even asked them yourself. You can count on your students to ask them.

Is it okay to ask these questions? Shouldn't we just have faith in God and not ask why? Some cultures believe that death and suffering are God's way of sorting and keeping the population in check. Does believing that really help?

YOU'LL NEED

- copy of **That's Not Fair!** (page 120), cut apart ahead of time
- whiteboard and dry erase marker
- Bibles
- copies of **Lifestyles of the Wicked and Famous** (page 121)
- pens or pencils
- copies of Habakkuk 3:17-19 for posting or distribution

This session explores these questions and reminds us of a key theme often described throughout the pages of Job. What's the answer you most commonly give? If you haven't experienced a time of deeper suffering yet, then you might not have wrestled as much with these issues. On the other hand, if you've been on the receiving end of deep pain and sorrow, then this theme may be all too real to you. Even so, you still may not have any good answers.

When struggling with a hard-hitting question such as, "Why don't the wicked suffer?" it's helpful to remember that the Bible is not to be understood in pieces alone. Biblical truths are to be understood in context and in light of the book as a whole. What else does the Bible say about the suffering of the righteous and the good?

Jesus quoted part of Psalm 22 while he hung on the cross. It's the tormented prayer of David who is wronged by the unwarranted attack of an enemy. David has not been delivered from this enemy yet. But if you were to read this psalm only through verse 21, you'd be left with a hopeless feeling. After reading verses 22 through 31, we begin to feel David's hope:

> I will declare your name to my brothers; in the congregation I will praise you. You who fear the Lord, praise him! All you descendants of Jacob, honor him! Revere him, all you descendants of Israel! For he has not despised or disdained the suffering of the afflicted one; he has not hidden his face from him but has listened to his cry for help. (vv. 22-24)

Even though life has been unfair, David declares his faith and hope in God who listens to his cry.

Romans 8, likewise, brings us words of hope. Beginning with verse 31 we read—

What, then, shall we say in response to this? If God is for us, who can be against us? He who did not spare his own Son, but gave him up for us all—how will he not also, along with him, graciously give us all things? Who will bring any charge against those whom God has chosen? It is God who justifies. Who is he that condemns? Christ Jesus, who died—more than that, who was raised to life—is at the right hand of God and is also interceding for us. Who shall separate us from the love of Christ? Shall trouble or hardship or persecution or famine or nakedness or danger or sword? As it is written: "For your sake we face death all day long; we are considered as sheep to be slaughtered." No, in all these things we are more than conquerors through him who loved us. For I am convinced that neither death nor life, neither angels nor demons, neither the present nor the future, nor any powers, neither height nor depth, nor anything else in all creation, will be able to separate us from the love of God that is in Christ Jesus our Lord. (8:31-39)

Before teaching this session, it will be important for you to consider your perspective, your experience, your response to the central theme of why God's loved ones suffer. Your attitude and understanding will inspire students to put their faith and trust in almighty God while continuing to seek their own responses and answers that work for them. It may be helpful, if possible, to spend time with someone who is suffering or has recently gone through a hard time. Your empathy for their circumstance will ground your own stance and awareness.

THE MAIN IDEA

We live in a world that brings us everything from great joy to deep suffering. Why do some people suffer more than others, especially those who've done nothing to deserve it? When the average Christian thinks of Job, suffering is often one of the themes they think of first. In this study students will "sit" with Job and try to understand why he's suffering, while the wicked seemingly enjoy life. And as they do so, they'll discover God's sovereignty and ultimate power over suffering and death.

FOR STARTERS

OPTION 1:

Begin this session by dividing your group into four or fewer teams, depending on the size of the group. Play the game "That's Not Fair!" using the page by the same name (page 120). The rules of the game are the same as the rules for Pictionary. Have one representative from each team come up and receive the situation from you. On the word *go*, each drawer will run back to their group and sketch out some clues on a sheet of paper or newsprint. The first team to yell out the answer receives a point. The team with the most points after 10 rounds wins. You could also give them nothing for winning, which would definitely seem unfair!

OPTION 2:

Ask your students to help you create a list of unfair circumstances in life. These could be either ones that affect them directly or affect others. Post the list on a whiteboard for all to see.

REFLECTION

Follow either one of these options with these questions:

- *What makes a situation unfair?*

- *In an unfair circumstance, does the party who benefits, in your opinion, enjoy the injustice because of the positive outcome or because they don't even consider that it might be wrong?*

- *What are some of our typical first responses to unjust situations?*

TRANSITION STATEMENT

Say something like—*In today's session, Job lets us read the diary of his feelings about the unjust circumstances in his life. He asks the question we so often ask, "Why does God allow the good to suffer?" This is a question that so many non-Christians raise as their reason for not following Christ. Our exploration of this passage will help us wrestle with this question and be reminded that God is ultimately in charge and the victor over sin and death.*

DISCOVER

Ask students to open their Bibles to Job 21, but first give this brief background—

Job's friend Zophar has just finished his speech, and for the sixth time Job responds to his friends. They've been talking about the horrible things that will happen to those who sin. The common perspective of the day was that the wicked always suffer. Job argues that while he isn't perfect, he certainly isn't wicked or deserving of the extreme suffering he's now experiencing. He also notes that the wicked actually enjoy seemingly prosperous lives. It's for this reason Job calls his friends to listen once more and then takes his complaint to God.

Distribute copies of **Lifestyles of the Wicked and Famous** (page 121) and something to write with. Give students an appropriate amount of time to complete most of the sheet with a partner. When they're finished, ask them to find another pair and compare answers.

When a reasonable amount of time has passed, reassemble the larger group and summarize by offering these questions:

  • *So what is Job's main point here?*

  • *After reading through his observations, complaints, and arguments, what are your initial feelings? Is he on target? Is he just too stressed to think clearly?*

  • *Does he have the right to complain?*

TRANSLATION, PLEASE!

This passage doesn't answer too many questions, and your students may be feeling a little uncomfortable. This section will help point students back to God as their authority.

Use the following true-or-false test as a way to logically help students see this troubling question in the context of God's truth. Allow your group to answer these verbally. Say—*True or false...*

  1. Job was human. (True—therefore, his perspective on

the good and the wicked could not have been perfect or always wise.)

2. Job believed that very few, if any, wicked people suffered as a result of their sins. (True—chapter 21 clearly shows his opinion.)

3. Job's friends believed, like many in their culture, that the wicked always suffer. (True—their arguments throughout the book of Job support this idea.)

4. No wicked people in the world have ever suffered. (False—observation of the world around us shows that suffering does not play favorites.)

5. There are very few stories in the Bible that show the consequences of those who sinned. (False—there are many stories throughout the Old Testament that show the direct results of people's sins. Noah and the ark is a great example. God's judgment on Sodom and Gomorrah is another, with many more that could be cited.)

Follow with these questions:

- *What do we do with Job's speech?*

- *Was Job purposely exaggerating? Or, given his circumstances, was this just the way Job saw life?*

- *How does this compare to us?* (When we're going through a rough time, it's easy to see life in a negative light.)

- *How did suffering come into the world?* (It began with Adam and Eve choosing to disobey God.)

- *What is God's role in times of injustice and suffering?*

- *What is the end of the story for those who walk with God and follow him in obedience?*

TRANSITION STATEMENT

Say something like—*God loves us so much that he sent his only Son to live among us on earth; here Jesus ultimately suffered and died for our sins. But he didn't just suffer and die; he also rose again to exhibit once and for all God's response to an unfair, unjust world where suffering is a part of the package. God doesn't like suffering any more than we do. Yet he promises to walk with us and that we'll have the ultimate victory over sadness, discouragement, separation, and death.*

MAKING IT WORK

Depending on the size of your group, ask students to either choose a partner or form a group of three. Invite all the groups to choose one person as the "sufferer" and then create a story about the situation that's causing the sufferer pain. The sufferers will then describe their circumstances to their partner(s), who will serve as the counselor(s). The counselor's role is to walk alongside the sufferer through this difficult time by helping the sufferer understand how God views suffering and how deep his love is for all people, even when they're suffering. Encourage the counselors to use all the ideas they gained through the study of this passage. After a little time has passed, have everyone switch roles and go through the role-play exercise again.

SO WHAT?

Habakkuk was a minor prophet who struggled with this same issue, yet he offered words of hope in Habakkuk 3:17-19. Before the session, you can either create a handout with this Scripture passage printed on it and make copies for all the students, or write the verses on a whiteboard for all to see:

> THOUGH THE FIG TREE DOES NOT BUD AND THERE ARE NO
> GRAPES ON THE VINES, THOUGH THE OLIVE CROP FAILS AND
> THE FIELDS PRODUCE NO FOOD, THOUGH THERE ARE NO
> SHEEP IN THE PEN AND NO CATTLE IN THE STALLS, YET I
> WILL REJOICE IN THE LORD. I WILL BE JOYFUL IN GOD MY
> SAVIOR. THE SOVEREIGN LORD IS MY STRENGTH; HE MAKES
> MY FEET LIKE THE FEET OF A DEER, HE ENABLES ME TO GO
> ON THE HEIGHTS.

Ask the group to read Habakkuk's words in unison.

Encourage your students by reminding them they aren't alone in their suffering. Those who follow Christ—and those who don't—all experience the consequences of a sinful world. Encourage them to support each other and depend on God for their hope and strength.

Close by offering students an opportunity to pray—silently or aloud—for one another to have strength and joy in the Lord.

THAT'S NOT FAIR!

Following are 10 unfair life situations. These are to be copied (according to the number of teams you have), cut apart, and distributed one-by-one at the beginning of each round of the game. Warn students that some of these examples are more abstract than others. Encourage them to take their time and help their team get started by guessing pieces of the circumstance first.

1. One basketball team has bigger players than the other team.

2. You enter the baseball stadium with your ticket, only to discover somebody is sitting in your high-priced seat and won't move.

3. Out of all the places to sit in the packed movie theatre, you find yourself seated in front of people who insist on offering a running commentary of the film.

4. You've been told you'll be paid a certain amount for completing a specific job. When you finish the job, you're only given half the promised amount.

5. Your parents punish you for something your little brother did.

6. You let your good friend borrow your digital camera. She drops it and breaks it.

7. Your friend put in one raffle ticket for a drawing, you put in ten. Your friend wins the raffle.

8. On the biggest night of your high school career—the prom—your date is sick and can't go.

9. People make fun of you because of your ethnicity.

10. After standing in a buffet line for 10 minutes, you finally reach your destination only to discover the food you wanted most is all gone.

LIFESTYLES OF THE WICKED AND FAMOUS

Read Job chapter 21 to complete the following chart.

Job's Big Question (v. 7)
The Benefits of Wicked Living (vv. 8-13)
Job's Three Questions about the Wicked…in Your Own Words (vv.17-18)   1)   2)   3)
Why the Wicked Seem to Win in the End (vv. 22-34)

LEADER PREP

The book of Job is found in the section of books we call Wisdom Literature. The other books of wisdom literature are Psalms, Proverbs, Ecclesiastes, and Song of Songs. The books of wisdom literature are characterized by their many references to wisdom and understanding. In the book of Job, the word *wisdom* is used 23 different times. The word *understanding* is found 14 times.

In the story of Solomon, we see how God honors those who seek wisdom. Solomon replaced his father, King David, on the throne of Israel. Seeing the godly example of his own dad, Solomon prayed these words,

YOU'LL NEED

- Mr. Bean video clip
- TV/DVD Player
- sheets of poster board or newsprint
- crayons or markers
- Bibles
- paper
- pens or pencils
- whiteboard and dry erase marker
- copies of **Where to Find Wisdom** (page 133)
- some type of container
- copies of **A Wisdom Planner** (page 134)

Now, O Lord my God, you have made your servant king in place of my father David. But I am only a little child and do not know how to carry out my duties. Your servant is here among the people you have chosen, a great people, too numerous to count or number. So give your servant a discerning heart to govern your people and to distinguish between right and wrong. For who is able to govern this great people of yours? (1 Kings 3:7-9)

Then in 1 Kings 3:10-15 we see the results of this prayer:

The Lord was pleased that Solomon had asked for this. So God said to him, "Since you have asked for this and not for long life or wealth for yourself, nor have asked for the death of your enemies but for discernment in administering justice, I will do what you have asked. I will give you a wise and discerning heart, so that there will never have been anyone like you, nor will there ever be. Moreover, I will give you what you have not asked for—both riches and honor—so that in your lifetime you will have no equal among kings. And if you walk in my ways and obey my statutes and commands as David your father did, I will give you a long life." Then Solomon awoke—and he realized it had been a dream.

In 1 Kings 4:29-34 the reward is explained even further: "God gave Solomon wisdom and very great insight, and a breadth of understanding as measureless as the sand on the seashore. Solomon's wisdom was greater than the wisdom of all the men of the East, and greater than all the wisdom of Egypt" (vv. 29-30).

In the New Testament, James declares the need for wisdom: "Who is wise and understanding among you? Let him show it by his good life, by deeds done in the humility that comes from wisdom" (James 3:13). Then James goes on to illustrate godly wisdom, "But the wisdom that comes from heaven is first of all pure; then peace-loving, considerate, submissive, full of mercy and good fruit, impartial and sincere" (James 3:17).

The study passage of this session focuses on the source of wisdom. Job asks, "But where can wisdom be found? Where does understanding dwell?" (Job 28:12). Note that Job is not asking about facts or knowledge. More information won't help his situation. He's already received plenty of information from his friends. Yet, he understands the value of God's wisdom to help him navigate these uncertain and extremely difficult times. Most importantly, Job recognizes that in order to have wisdom, one must fear the Lord (Job 28:28).

Your role in this session is to help students appreciate and recognize the role of wisdom in their lives. It's not always about answering one more question or having one more piece of information. Seek God for understanding and wisdom as you prepare for this time.

THE MAIN IDEA

We live in a world where having information seems to be everything. "The more you know" is a creed of many. This study focuses on something deeper. Job delivers a speech that asks the question, "Where can wisdom be found? Where does understanding dwell?" In this session students will discover the difference between wisdom and knowledge. They'll ask the same question as Job and uncover God's answer to us.

FOR STARTERS

OPTION 1:

Ahead of time, either rent or buy a Mr. Bean (played by Rowan Atkinson) DVD and choose a clip to play for your group. (You can either find Mr. Bean videos at most rental stores or purchase them on the Internet.) Even the simplest tasks of daily life can be a difficult challenge for Mr. Bean; but in the end, he always finds a way—usually a humorous one—to resolve the problem.

Show one of the Mr. Bean stories. A few of the classics include his adventures at church or at the dentist's office. As always, preview any clip before showing it to your youth group. Most Mr. Bean clips are appropriate for all ages, but you're the best judge of what works with your group.

OPTION 2:

Begin by asking your students the following questions: *When I say the words* absent-minded professor, *how would you describe such a person? What do we know about professors? Why would they be absent-minded?*

Have students offer other examples (without using names) of people they know who possess incredible intelligence but lack practical or common sense skills in certain areas.

REFLECTION

Introduce the following questions as a way to reflect on one of the two previous options:

• *What's the difference between wisdom and knowledge?* (Knowledge is the accumulation of information; wisdom is the practical, day-to-day application of knowledge.)

• *How was that difference shown in the examples we heard or saw?*

• *What are some ways we can get knowledge?*

• *How do we get wisdom?*

• *If you could choose only one, would you rather have knowledge or wisdom? Why?*

TRANSITION STATEMENT

Say something like—*Our world values the collection of information. People enjoy impressing each other with their memorized facts about famous people, places, technology, and so on. While it's important to be knowledgeable (especially during that test for third period!), there's much more to life than knowing a bunch of facts. How long do you remember the information you crammed into your head for that last exam? Today we find Job giving his sixth speech and asking the question, "Where can wisdom be found?" We'll discover what he says about this topic and explore the answer God longs for us to hear.*

DISCOVER

Today's session is really a lesson about a lesson. Job has masterfully given us a teaching within chapter 28. For our purposes it will be divided this way:

1) Hidden riches (vv. 1-11)

2) Wisdom isn't for sale (vv. 12-19)

3) Wisdom is found in God (vv. 20-28)

In each section of this passage, students will be offered a different exercise to bring the words to life.

HIDDEN RICHES (28:1-11)

Ask students to form groups of three to five people. Give each group a sheet of poster board or a large piece of newsprint and a set of markers or crayons. Request that one student from each group read the passage while the others follow along in their own Bibles. After the reading is completed, the students should draw what they've just heard. Some students may have more artistic ability than others—that's okay. Reassure them this isn't an art contest, but a way for them to see what Job is presenting. Invite them to be creative and allow everyone in each group to contribute something to the creation. Play some background music and enjoy walking around your art studio!

After an appropriate amount of time, bring all the groups back together and have them present their artwork and explain why they placed certain drawings in specific locations.

To summarize, ask—*If there were nothing else to this passage, what would you have learned so far?*

WISDOM ISN'T FOR SALE (VV. 12-19)

Invite students to return to their small groups, and give each group a sheet of paper and something to write with. One person will read aloud this portion of the chapter, and then the group will collectively create a list of all the precious materials that cannot buy wisdom. Next to each item, have them describe or identify any known characteristics about the material.

Bring the groups back together, compare lists, and recap with this question: *What simple yet profound truth do these verses give us about how we gain wisdom?* (We can't buy it, we can't go to a seminar to obtain it, and hiring the best tutor in the world won't bring us more wisdom.) List their ideas on a whiteboard.

WISDOM IS FOUND IN GOD (VV. 20-28)

Ask your students go back to their groups one more time and read the final verses of this chapter together. They could read them silently or go around the circle, each reading one verse until they're finished.

Distribute copies of **Where to Find Wisdom** (page 133)—one to each group—and have them work together to complete the page. When the groups are finished, gather them back together to share their results.

TRANSLATION, PLEASE!

Begin this section by asking the question—*What does it mean to fear the Lord?* After you've allowed a few students to offer their definitions, say—*The phrase* fear the Lord *is found 22 times in the Bible. This behavior may be a result of wisdom, but what does it really mean to fear God?*

To help your students think through this definition, have them take a sheet of paper and tear it into about eight different pieces. On each piece, have them write down one thing they—or other people—are afraid of. After all the students have done this, collect the slips of paper in a hat, jar, or can and stir them up. Divide your group into two teams and send the teams to opposite sides of the room.

The object of this game is to guess as many of the written items as possible in 30 seconds. Team A will select one person to give the clues. The clue-giver will randomly select pieces of paper, one-by-one, and offer clues about as many different fears as they can in the time allotted. Meanwhile, their team will guess the fears by shouting out their answers until the correct one is given. Similar to the rules for the game called *Taboo*, the clue-giver can describe the item using any words he desires, except those that rhyme with the answer or include part or all of the words written on the paper. If the clue-giver is clueless and wants to skip one of the items, he may do so; but one point will be taken away from his team for every item skipped.

When the 30 seconds are up, Team B will have their chance. This contest will go back and forth for as many rounds as you choose. The team with the most points wins.

At the end of the competition, present these questions:

> • *How would you define the type of fear referred to in this game?*
>
> • *Do you believe this is the type of fear Job was proposing? Why or why not?*

Use the following definition to further express the true definition of *fear* in this passage: Easton's 1897 Bible Dictionary *describes* fear of the Lord *as "a fear conjoined with love and hope." Therefore, it's not the type of fear where we dread, but rather reverence our loving God.* (www.biblegateway.com/resources/dictionaries)

MAKING IT WORK

Introduce this part of the session by once again reading Job 28:28. Then ask, *What is wisdom?* and *What is understanding?*

Distribute copies of **A Wisdom Planner** (page 134) to each student. Go over the directions and then set them free to do their work.

After you've given your students ample time to complete the project, bring them back together and reflect on the activity with these questions:

- *What did you learn about yourself from this exercise?*

- *At what time of day do you seem to be the strongest and at what time of day do you seem to be the weakest?*

- *How would you rate the challenge of actually implementing this? Extremely challenging? Somewhat challenging? A little challenging? Easy?*

SO WHAT?

As you close today, remind students wisdom can only be found when they put Christ first in their lives. Without calling upon God, their search for wisdom will be futile. This requires a sincere prayer for wisdom throughout their days. As students do this, God will honor their prayers and provide the wisdom they need.

Finish the session with a guided prayer. Begin by asking God to give your students the desire to pray for wisdom. Then pray for their morning, afternoon, and nighttime activities. For each part of the day you mention, pause so students may specifically pray for wisdom in their individual areas. Complete the prayer by asking God to use each person to encourage others to honor God in all they do.

WHERE TO FIND WISDOM

Using Job 28:20-28 as your guide, please complete the following:

According to verse 20, the big questions are—

1)

2)

Verse	Characteristics of Wisdom
21	
22	
23	
27	
27	
27	
28	

A WISDOM PLANNER

Below is a grid outlining a schedule for your day. Think through the different elements of an average day and try to think of ways you could intentionally strive to fear God and shun evil in your daily activities. If you have events that cross over from one time span to the next, just assign the event to one or the other. For example, if basketball practice begins at 4 p.m. and ends at 6 p.m., then assign basketball to the 3 p.m. to 5 p.m. time slot.

Here's an example to get you started:

6 a.m. – 8 a.m.   Read two chapters in the Bible
                        Pray for five minutes
                        Don't turn on the TV

Time of Day	Wisdom Strategy
6 a.m. – 8 a.m.	
8 a.m. – noon	
noon – 1 pm.	
1 pm. - 3 pm.	
3 pm. - 5 pm.	
5 pm. - 7 pm.	
7 pm. – 9 p.m.	
9 p.m. – midnight	

HOW TO SURVIVE SUFFERING—LETTING GOD BE GOD

LEADER PREP

Being in the presence of someone with a "take-charge" attitude can be an interesting experience. It could be a very positive encounter, or it could be very negative. On the positive side, most people would say they love being led by someone who has planned well and leads them along. If you've ever had the opportunity to be under the leadership of a good director at a conference or to follow a good tour guide during a trip, then you're familiar with the feeling. In this environment you have very few worries. You're given an itinerary, your transportation awaits you, the restaurants are already chosen, and special sites are selected in advance. When you contrast this with having to make all the choices on your own, it's easy to feel spoiled by a good tour guide.

YOU'LL NEED

- copies of **Tour Guide** (page 145)
- pens or pencils
- clip from *Bruce Almighty*
- Bibles
- whiteboard and dry erase marker
- copies of **God Is God (and I Am Not)** (page 146)
- copies of **Wondering About God** (page 147)

On the negative side, there are few events more agonizing than when you're being directed by someone who micromanages, overextends her power, and manipulates the activities in a way that neither listens to the desires of the followers nor ultimately cares if they're happy with the way things are going.

When circumstances in our lives fall apart around us, our sinful default setting is "I'm taking back control." It seems apparent that God cares about us—but maybe he doesn't care enough to do anything about our situation. So we seek ways to make our lives better, we seek quick cures, we look for books with the answers, we seek the opinions of other humans, and more. Whatever it takes to make the hurt go away, we'll do it. We feel as though God has left the building on this one, and now we're in charge.

As Job sits and listens to his friends, we might wonder if he thinks God has gone on vacation. The sound of their misguided advice seems to drone on and on. We might wonder if Job begins believing their hollow counsel. His friends see the pain; they see the tragedy; and they seek to fix it. Sure, it appears they also love God, but in a way that only sees a mere glimpse of the God who made the universe and would ultimately prove his love for a sinful people in a way not yet imagined.

It would be fair to guess that Job must have been tempted to take matters into his own hands. Day after day he felt the loss and heard the biting words. Who wouldn't have considered saying, "Enough already!" We know Job couldn't replace all the lives lost or the possessions destroyed, but the temptation to do something—as opposed to just waiting—could have been bigger than we realize.

As we'll see in this study, Job knew better. His practice of being faithful to God, of being "blameless and upright," one who "feared God and shunned evil" (Job 1:1) present-ed him with the foundation of a strong relationship with God. Though the temptation was there, Job's faith would not be compromised because Job knew the greatness and majesty of the all-knowing, all-loving, and just God.

In preparing to teach this session, take time to immerse yourself in the great works of God among his people. As you walk around outside, take in the glory of his creation in the night sky, in the varieties of plants, the uniqueness of the animals, and the exact position of the earth in the solar system that allows you not to burn up or freeze. Be aware of your body in a new way! Stop for a moment and wonder how your tongue works or how your eyes allow you to see colors or how all your senses function to receive signals that are interpreted by your brain for storage and appli-cation. Recognize the complexity of your body's systems, which allows you to do so many tasks that you probably take for granted.

Ponder the vast power of God in the lives of people through the Old and New Testaments. You could spend a lifetime comprehending all of this!

Let the words of Psalm 8 enthuse you as you get ready to lead your students on a discovery of our God:

> O Lord, our Lord,
> how majestic is your name in all the earth!
> You have set your glory
> above the heavens.
>
> From the lips of children and infants
> you have ordained praise
> because of your enemies,
> to silence the foe and the avenger.

When I consider your heavens,
the work of your fingers,
the moon and the stars,
which you have set in place,

what is man that you are mindful of him,
the son of man that you care for him?

You made him a little lower than the heavenly beings
and crowned him with glory and honor.

You made him ruler over the works of your hands;
you put everything under his feet:

all flocks and herds,
and the beasts of the field,

the birds of the air,
and the fish of the sea,
all that swim the paths of the seas.

O Lord, our Lord,
how majestic is your name in all the earth!

THE MAIN IDEA

Through sin, suffering came into the world, and now we can count on experiencing it in one form or another. While people respond to suffering in different ways, no one would claim to enjoy it. Today's session seeks to help students answer the question of how they might best respond to the pain through their recognition of our God who "can do all things."

FOR STARTERS

OPTION 1:

Begin today's session by calling on your students to find a travel agent partner. Distribute **Tour Guide** (page 145) and give students about 10 minutes (or more if needed) to complete the project. Play some fun background music while the students work.

OPTION 2:

Rent or purchase the movie *Bruce Almighty* (starring Jim Carrey). Be aware that some parents or even some students may not be comfortable with the premise of this movie, where a human is given God's powers for a limited time. However, if you choose to use a clip from the film, you'll find scenes to give your students a sense of what it might be like to be God on any given day. Preview the movie ahead of time and look for scenes that will communicate this idea, but use your discretion, making sure the scenes you choose won't get you into trouble if you show them to your students.

REFLECTION FOR OPTION 1

Bring the travel agency partnerships back together and have each pair give a summary presentation of their trip. Follow up with these questions:

- *How many of you enjoyed planning this tour?*
- *What do you need to know about a destination to help you plan a quality tour?*

- *What do you need to know about the travelers?*

- *For those who've actually gone on a tour before, what was the best thing about having somebody else in charge?*

- *What's the downside of having somebody else in charge?*

REFLECTION FOR OPTION 2

- *What's appealing about actually being given the power of God?*

- *What would be the downside of receiving all the power of God?*

- *What percentage of people, in your opinion, would want to have all the power of God, just so they could be in charge of everything?*

TRANSITION STATEMENT

Say something like—*There are times when we love taking care of the details and knowing what's going to happen next. Other times we love having someone take care of us. And there are still other times when somebody else is in charge, but we'd prefer to be the ones calling the shots. Job was in just such a time. Suffering and pain were controlling his life and there was no end in sight. Job recognized God as his Creator, he recognized God's love for him, and in this passage we discover Job's declaration of a God who is in control. Through this session we'll discover how to survive our times of suffering by acknowledging God's complete and loving control of our world and our lives.*

DISCOVER

Chapter 42 of Job begins with his final answer to God. Throughout these sessions we've walked with Job through the suffering, his questions to God, the less-than-helpful advice of his friends, and now we come to his final response.

Ask your students to open their Bibles to chapter 42. Invite your best reader to read the first six verses, then discuss the following questions as a group:

• *What confessions does Job make in these verses?* (List these answers on a whiteboard so the whole group can see.)

• *What does it mean that no plan of God's can be thwarted?* (verse 2)

• *Job spoke of things he didn't understand. When was the last time you did this?* (Come ready with an example from your own life.)

• *What happens when we finally see something we've only heard about?* (verse 5)

• *What was Job's final, nonverbal response before God in verse 6?* (Tell the students that dust and ashes are symbolic of humiliation and insignificance. Abraham first mentions this in Genesis 18:27.)

TRANSLATION, PLEASE!

Say something like—*The words of Job 38-40 mark God's appearance to Job. Out of the storm (38:1) God answers Job, and his words are mighty. God speaks of his amazing creation in a straightforward and detailed manner. These chapters provide a context for Job's response as we have been studying in this session. Let God overwhelm you with his power.*

Recruit some of your best readers to read, with feeling, large portions or all the verses of Job 38-40 (if you have time). You could have them be seated in front or in a prominent place on stools or chairs. Be sure everybody is reading from the same version and consider dividing the readings into 10 verses each. If you choose to read only portions of these chapters, take time before the session to determine the exact verses.

After the reading say something like—*Job recognizes that God is—well, God—and Job is not. In our heads we probably know this is true, but how do we translate Job's confessions into our own world? How do we let God be God, accept God's "big picture" understanding of our lives, live with God's hard decisions even when we're not happy with the outcome? This next exercise helps us compare our humanness to God's majesty, mighty power, and desire for us to experience his best.*

Distribute copies of **God Is God (and I Am Not)** (page 146) to your students. If you have the space, encourage them to find a comfortable place to work individually for the next 15 minutes. Introduce this as a time when they can be quiet before God and let him speak to them. No words are required. Dismiss your group and participate in the activity yourself.

Once the time has ended (feel free to add or subtract time, depending on the nature of your group), bring the group back together. Before you move on to the next section, share how this is one of those exercises that looks good on paper but is actually more challenging to apply in real life.

MAKING IT WORK

Debrief their individual work time by asking the following reflective question—*What are some reasons why you believe you can trust God?* (List these up front for your students.)

In **Wondering About God** (page 147), there are three case studies describing people who are experiencing pain in their lives. Choose three students to present one case study each—as it's written and in the first person—and give them a copy of **Wondering About God**. After the study is presented, ask the group to help each person walk through the process of letting God be God. The case study person should then be allowed to respond.

Your role is the moderator—keep the conversation authentic and easily understood on both sides. Don't let students get away with cliché statements such as, "I guess God needed her more than we did." When you feel the dialogue has come to a fitting end, ask everyone to reflect on the experience. What went right? What went wrong? Help them understand there isn't always a final answer.

SO WHAT?

By now your students are realizing how difficult it is to survive a time of suffering by letting God be in control and by putting their trust in him. Let them know their feelings are very real. Challenge them to keep that perspective when they respond to others who are broken by pain and difficult times. Dare them to spend more time listening to and walking with their friends through the dark times, rather than trying to answer why.

As you close today, ask willing students to briefly share any situations in which they find themselves—either personally or through their friends—where there seem to be no answers but plenty of questions. Ask different students to offer a one- or two-sentence prayer for each shared situation, and then close with a prayer for everybody.

TOUR GUIDE

You and your partner have recently formed a travel agency. You, like anybody else, want to succeed. On the opening day of the agency, you receive a phone call. A wealthy client wants to take a trip with 11 other people for seven days to the place of your choice. You question the client further, as you can't believe he's actually letting you decide his destination. But he insists that he's serious.

Your assignment is to put together a tour that leaves from your hometown, arrives at the destination, and then returns back home. You'll be in charge of everything from the moment the group leaves to the moment they return. With the help of the planning sheet below, form a profile for this tour.

Name of Your Travel Agency: _____

Destination(s): _____

Duration: 7 days

Cost (include travel, lodging, food, and entertainment events): _____

Daily Schedule

Day 1 —

Day 2 —

Day 3 —

Day 4 —

Day 5 —

Day 6 —

Day 7 —

GOD IS GOD (AND I AM NOT)

Using this worksheet, take some time to ponder who God is in contrast with who you are. This is a solo effort, so make yourself comfortable and let God speak personally to you. (Go back and review God's eye-opening response to Job in chapters 38 through 40 for extra insights!)

TEN THINGS GOD CAN DO THAT I CAN'T

1. _____
2. _____
3. _____
4. _____
5. _____
6. _____
7. _____
8. _____
9. _____
10. _____

ONE THING I CAN DO THAT GOD CAN'T

1. _____

FIVE WAYS WE SEEM TO SUFFER MOST IN LIFE

1. _____
2. _____
3. _____
4. _____
5. _____

FIVE WAYS GOD COULD PREVENT OR ERASE THESE AREAS OF SUFFERING

1. _____
2. _____
3. _____
4. _____
5. _____

TWO FACTS I KNOW ABOUT GOD FROM JOB 42:2

1. _____
2. _____

THREE REASONS WHY I CAN TRUST GOD'S BIG-PICTURE PLAN FOR MY LIFE

1. _____
2. _____
3. _____

WONDERING ABOUT GOD

CASE #1

Hi, my name is Derek. I moved to this town about five years ago. Our family moved here because we were told life was going to be better for my dad with his new job. Life was better for a while. My dad really enjoyed his new job, my sister and I found some good friends, and my mom seemed happier than ever. Then everything came crashing down. My dad was called into the office and told that, due to economic problems, he was going to be laid off—immediately. Not too long after that, a few of my closest friends learned this was happening to their parents as well. Their parents quickly found employment elsewhere and moved. We're stuck here, without good friends, no income from my dad, and now there seems to be more tension between my parents. When we left the last place five years ago, my parents believed God was leading us here for a reason. I don't see the reason. Where is God? Doesn't he care anymore?

CASE #2

My name is Kendra. If you see me at school and talk to me at lunch or between classes, you might think I'm one of the nicest and happiest people you know. And if you think that, then you'd be half right. I am a nice person, or at least I try to be. But for the most part, I'm not happy because I feel as though I don't have anything to offer. I don't play an instrument; I don't sing; I'm not good at any sports; my reading ability is average; and my grades are just so-so. When there's potential for me to be selected for anything, I'm pretty sure I either won't get chosen or I'll be chosen last. I can't remember the last time I received a compliment from anybody, including my parents. Don't worry. I'm not going to do something bad to myself. I just don't feel very happy. I know the Bible says God loves us all and has given us each special gifts. What's my gift? I think he's forgotten about me.

CASE #3

Hey, my name is Chase. I've been a Christian for almost all of my 17 years. My parents are Christians and they've been a great example to me for what it means to love and obey Christ. My sisters and I feel very loved by them. We have a great church, and we're all very involved with different ministries. We even help a lot in the community. So, life is going well for me, right? Well, no! When I was little, I was diagnosed with cystic fibrosis. While there are many new treatments, there is no known cure. I will likely die at a young age. Many have asked me if this disease is in my family history, and the answer is no. I'm the lucky one! So, I can't even answer the question, "Why me?" It came out of nowhere. Yeah, I've been a lot of help to other people as they've seen my strength and perseverance, but what about me? I know what the Bible says about eternal life, but what about life right now? I have so much more to do. I know God has a bigger purpose for me than just these short years. Why won't he miraculously heal me?

THE REWARDS OF PASSING THE SUFFERING TEST

SESSION 12: JOB 42:7-17

LEADER PREP

What is the best material reward you've ever received? When we think from a spiritual perspective (as you may be doing right now) the word *reward* is often defined in these terms: eternal life, a lasting or healthy relationship, the love of others, etc. The Bible encourages us to focus on these, but again we ask, "What is the best material reward you've ever received?" Was it a cash prize from a contest? Was it the opportunity to go on a trip? Was it a new car? Was it an unexpected cash bonus for hard work? Fill in the blank. Most likely we've all won something or been rewarded for our actions. Those were happy moments for us, even if the glory soon passed.

The upside of rewards is their encouragement to us. Good things *can* happen! If the reward was received in direct connection to our

YOU'LL NEED

- copies of **Famous Prizes** (page 157)
- pens or pencils
- whiteboard and dry erase marker
- copies of **Job's Rewards** (page 158)
- poster board or sheets of poster paper for each group
- markers for each group
- copies of **Blessing Dilemmas** (pages 159-160)

actions or work, then we're motivated to continue the excellence.

The downside of rewards is our renewed expectation of receiving them as a direct result of our good work. Do you remember the last time you did something nice or extra for someone and received no appreciation or gratitude? How did it feel? John Wooden, the great former coach of the UCLA Bruin basketball team once said, "You cannot live a perfect day without doing something for someone who will never be able to repay you" (*They Call Me Coach*, Word Books, 1972). This sounds great. We might even like to live this out, yet we struggle when the rewards don't arrive when we feel they should.

The story of Job ends with him receiving the bonus of having the second part of his life blessed more than the first. As we've worked through these sessions, it'd be natural for us to assess that this is the *least* he should have received. However, we know the end result of pain doesn't always include rewards. We can think of many faithful Christians who've suffered tremendous losses, kept their faith strong, yet never saw any kind of reward.

The book of Jeremiah displays for us a great picture of a devoted servant of God who never saw a reward in his life or ministry. Jeremiah was a priest. He was commanded to not marry or raise children because of God's coming judgment on Judah. Jeremiah's calling was to announce the destruction of the kingdom of Judah. He's often been called the "weeping prophet." The book of Jeremiah chronicles his life and suffering for this call. The book of Lamentations further expounds on the hardship he experienced in the midst of being faithful to God. Would we do the same?

This final study of Job's life reveals God's final response. God responds to Job's friends first, and then he responds to Job's unwavering relationship to him. Job receives an amazing and overwhelming blessing from God. Nowhere in this book does it suggest Job knew it was coming. Job persistently clings to the hope he has in God. He knows of no guarantees in life, but he knows the God who is the Author of true life. May this hope be at the center of your life, as you teach the good news of God's greatest reward to your students.

THE MAIN IDEA

Despite the worst of circumstances, Job remained faithful to God. In the end God restores his possessions and gives him more children. In this session students will discover that fully trusting God ultimately results in experiencing God's unceasing love through his gift of eternal life.

FOR STARTERS

OPTION 1:

Use the multiple-choice trivia test **Famous Prizes** (page 157) to begin this session. You can either make copies to distribute, read the questions aloud so students can answer in teams, or develop the quiz into a PowerPoint game to be played by the teams. The answers are: 1) c; 2) a; 3) b; 4) a; 5) b; 6) a; 7) c; 8) b; 9) b; 10) b.

OPTION 2:

Begin this session by asking students to share about some of the interesting rewards they've earned or won. Ask them to describe what led up to the reward, how the reward was presented, and the nature of the reward.

REFLECTION

Follow either option with these questions:

- *Why do rewards motivate us to work for something?*
- *When is a reward not helpful?*
- *How are rewards abused by those who give them?*
- *Have you ever received a reward for something you didn't do? How did that feel?*
- *What is ultimately most rewarding for you?*

TRANSITION STATEMENT

Say something like—*As we come to the end of Job, we find him finishing the most horrible days of his life. Job has just completed his final response to God, and now God responds— first to Job's friends and then to Job. In God's response we learn a lot about God's character. While we'd certainly agree that Job deserves the reward he ultimately receives from God, we'll discover how God sees the "big picture" and from that perspective he offers us the very best kind of reward.*

DISCOVER

Invite one of your students to read aloud Job 42:7-9. God has allowed Job's friends to preach at Job for a while, but now God steps to the front. Ask your students to imagine what it would be like to be one of Job's friends. Ask them what they'd be feeling right now—confidence? Insecurity? Conviction?

Follow up with these questions:

- *Why should the friends feel guilty?*
- *What is significant about Job praying for his friends as they offer their sacrifices to God?*
- *What statement appears twice in this passage—about what the friends have done and how they've acted in comparison to Job?*

Divide your students into smaller groups of three to five people. Distribute **Job's Rewards** (page 158), as well as poster board or poster-size paper and markers to each group. Encourage students to take the next several minutes and read Job 42:10-17. After reading through the passage, their assignment is to complete the project on this page.

TRANSLATION, PLEASE!

When a majority of the groups have finished, bring them back together to work through the meaning of this study. Begin by having each group display their picture for the larger group to see. For those who chose to draw a more symbolic picture, ask them to describe their representation of God's blessings upon Job.

After the presentations, offer these questions for reflection and translation:

- *At what point did God decide to make Job prosperous again?*

• Some people believe our faithful prayers directly result in consistent physical rewards. How would you prove that to be true using the evidence found in these verses?

• How would you disprove this with other stories from the Old and New Testaments?

• Is God required to reward us because we are faithful to him in our actions, thoughts, and prayers?

• How do you believe God normally operates?

• In verse 10, it says God gave Job twice as much as he had before. In verse 16, it says Job lived to 140 years old, which was twice the number of years for a normal person in those times. What does this say about how God blesses us?

• Why is it better to worship a God who chooses to bless us, rather than one who's required *to bless us?*

MAKING IT WORK

By this point in the study, you've possibly stirred up some controversy. There may be some who believe God always provides physical blessings and rewards for those who are faithful. There will be others who wonder if God ever really blesses those who are faithful—while they're still living on earth anyway. These students may have personally experienced—either firsthand or through friends and extended family members—what it means to struggle through life and receive very little reward, even though it could be argued they really deserved one. The third group of students will be those who fall somewhere in between. The bottom line is that sometimes God blesses us with earthly rewards and sometimes he doesn't.

If there are different perspectives about God's response represented in your group, encourage students to learn from one another and keep the discussion going. No human knows exactly how God works and responds. We all must respond in faith that God knows us, loves us, and ultimately wants the best for us. With this in mind, challenge your students to think about how they wrestle with this idea in their own lives and in the lives of others.

Ask students to return to their smaller groups. Distribute **Blessing Dilemmas** (pages 159-160) and give them an appropriate amount of time to work on it before bringing them together for the second half of the task.

After the groups are all back together, pair them up and have them do the following:

• Group A reads their case study to Group B. Group B responds by answering these questions: *How would you help this person keep a balanced perspective on God's choice to bless? How would you celebrate with the person over this amazing answer to prayer, while still helping them understand this may not be the way God will answer in every instance?*

• Start all groups at the same time. Give them a set amount of time and then end the exercise when the time is up.

• Now Group B reads their case study (from the same category) and Group A responds.

• Repeat this process for the other two categories.

• If you need to combine an odd number of groups, then two groups can combine to respond to another group's case study.

SO WHAT?

Students may still have questions about how God chooses to respond when we've faithfully passed the test of suffering, pain, or challenge. Encourage them to remember there are no easy answers. Only with faith is there the ability to persevere and look forward to victory—either in this world or in the next.

As a fitting end to this entire study, ask students to stand. Post the words of Job 19:23-27 on a whiteboard and ask them to read these key verses in unison.

After the reading, pray a prayer of blessing over your group, asking God to help them understand and receive the true blessings and rewards he has for them now and for eternity.

FAMOUS PRIZES

For certain events people win unique prizes. Take a look at these questions and guess what special prize the winner receives. Circle the letter next to your answer.

1. At the Kentucky Derby, a fast horse races around an oval track with a very light person on its back. Besides money, what's the prize?

a. A big cube of sugar for the horse

b. A special saddle

c. A garland of roses

2. Those who write well receive a prestigious award for their work. This prize is called the—

a. Pulitzer Prize

b. *New York Times* Achievement Award

c. Gold Medallion

3. The Nobel Prize is awarded for achievements in what categories?

a. Peace, mathematics, environment, medicine, economics, and literature

b. Physics, chemistry, peace, medicine, economics, and literature

c. Peace, science, genetic engineering, chemistry, business, economics, and literature

4. The Caldecott Medal is awarded for what area of children's literature?

a. Illustration

b. Writing

c. Creative book cover

5. If you win a Razzie Award, should you receive it as a compliment or a slap in the face?

a. Compliment

b. Slap in the face

6. The Clio Award is given to those who create the best what?

a. Advertising pieces for radio, television, or print

b. Special feature news story for radio

c. Magazine cover

7. People who write horror stories annually win the Stoker Award. This award is in the shape of what?

a. A vampire

b. A werewolf

c. A haunted mansion

8. The Astral Award is annually given for what achievement?

a. Outer space research

b. Web site design

c. Astrology presentation

9. Comics creators annually look forward to receiving one of what series of awards?

a. The Schulz Awards

b. The Harvey Awards

c. The Funny Awards

10. The Stevie Award is given for the best of what category?

a. Women entrepreneurs

b. Business executives

c. Airline pilots

JOB'S REWARDS

In your small group, read through Job 42:10-17 and complete the following:

Verse	What Job Gained
10	
11	
12	
13	
16	
17	

Using the markers and poster paper, work together as a group and draw a picture of Job's rewards. Your drawing can be either symbolic or literal in its representation of God's blessings to Job.

BLESSING DILEMMAS

Though we live faithfully for God, we're still citizens of a fallen world where sin, injustice, and suffering are a part of our lives—in the past, present, or future. In times of great pain or need, many have prayed and either received miraculous answers, received no answer, or experienced life getting worse. You've probably experienced a few of these answers directly or in the lives of your family and friends.

Your assignment is to produce one case study for each of the categories below. These case studies could be a real-life, first-person experience or based on the experience of someone you know. If you choose to create a story, please keep it based in reality—an experience you might actually encounter.

After each group has generated case studies, the whole group will come together and respond to these situations.

GOD'S DIRECT REWARD OR BLESSING IN RESPONSE TO A SPECIFIC PRAYER

(e.g., Blaine's family is hurting. Blaine just lost his job, and his wife is sick. They hardly have enough money to put food on the table. Blaine and his wife faithfully pray for God to provide for them. The very next day some unexpected gift certificates from an anonymous donor arrive in the mail. With these certificates, Blaine's family will be able to buy groceries for a week.)

Your Case Study:

GOD'S NON-ANSWER TO A SPECIFIC PRAYER

(e.g., Judy just found out her grandmother has a terminal illness. Judy's grandmother is a strong, Christian woman who deeply loves her family and her church. Many people, including Judy, have diligently prayed for her healing, but now the doctors have given her only days to live.)

Your Case Study:

GOD ALLOWS LIFE TO GET WORSE—EVEN AFTER YOU SPECIFICALLY PRAYED FOR THE OPPOSITE RESULT

(e.g., Roberto's dad recently announced he was seeking a divorce from Roberto's mom. Roberto shared this news with his youth pastor, and many people in the youth ministry prayed for their reconciliation. Roberto wanted more than anything for them to stay together. After weeks of prayer, there seemed to be no resolution in sight. Then one evening the phone rings and Roberto hears more bad news: His best friend is moving to another city.)

Your Case Study: